AGRICULTURAL AND ENVIRONMENTAL POLICY INTEGRATION:

Recent Progress and New Directions

ORGANISATION FOR ECONOMIC CO-OPERATION AND DEVELOPMENT

ORGANISATION FOR ECONOMIC CO-OPERATION AND DEVELOPMENT

Pursuant to Article 1 of the Convention signed in Paris on 14th December 1960, and which came into force on 30th September 1961, the Organisation for Economic Co-operation and Development (OECD) shall promote policies designed:

— to achieve the highest sustainable economic growth and employment and a rising standard of living in Member countries, while maintaining financial stability, and thus to contribute to the development of the world economy;

— to contribute to sound economic expansion in Member as well as non-member countries in the process of economic development; and

— to contribute to the expansion of world trade on a multilateral, non-discriminatory basis in accordance with international obligations.

The original Member countries of the OECD are Austria, Belgium, Canada, Denmark, France, Germany, Greece, Iceland, Ireland, Italy, Luxembourg, the Netherlands, Norway, Portugal, Spain, Sweden, Switzerland, Turkey, the United Kingdom and the United States. The following countries became Members subsequently through accession at the dates indicated hereafter: Japan (28th April 1964), Finland (28th January 1969), Australia (7th June 1971) and New Zealand (29th May 1973). The Commission of the European Communities takes part in the work of the OECD (Article 13 of the OECD Convention).

Publié en français sous le titre :

L'INTÉGRATION DES POLITIQUES DE L'AGRICULTURE
ET DE L'ENVIRONNEMENT :
Progrès récents et nouvelles orientations

Foreword

Agriculture has always been very closely associated with the environment. This association is reflected by, for example, the production of high quality food and fibre, the habitation of the countryside helping to maintain the vitality and diversity of rural communities, maintenance of the landscape and habitats, the provision of recreational facilities and environmental protection.

In the last decade a growing concern has emerged about the consequences of some agricultural practices and policies that indirectly encourage negative environmental impacts. At the same time there has been increased awareness of the impact on the agriculture sector and the productivity of the land base arising from a reduction in environmental quality caused by non-agricultural activities.

OECD governments recognise that sustainable agriculture requires, inter alia, the integration of agriculture and environment policies. In an effort to implement policy integration, an increasingly wider range of policy instruments are being employed, administrative structures and legislation are being revised and redefined, and the relationship between environmental quality, and input and output factors of production is receiving greater scrutiny.

This report is a review of progress made in agricultural and environmental policy integration over the period 1988-1990. The report first examines concepts relevant to the agriculture and environment policy integration discussion. Following this, and based on a survey of OECD countries, a review of recently proposed and enacted policy integration measures is presented. Finally, new directions and priorities are identified to provide guidance for another phase of study that would extend the present work.

The report is the result of a study carried out by the ad hoc Group on Agriculture and the Environment. It has been approved by the Agriculture Committee and the Environment Policy Committee and is published on the responsibility of the Secretary-General of the OECD.

The contributions of David Baldock, Institute for European Environmental Policy (London), and David Ervin, Oregon State University, in the preparation of this report are gratefully acknowledged.

ALSO AVAILABLE

Agricultural and Environmental Policies : Opportunities for Integration (1989)
(97 88 04 1) ISBN 92-64-13127-2   FF100   £12.00   US$22.00   DM43

Agricultural Policies, Markets and Trade: Monitoring and Outlook 1992 (1992)
(51 92 04 1) ISBN 92-64-13655-X   FF215   £28.00   US$50.00   DM84

Market and Government Failures in Environmental Management: Wetlands and Forests (1992)
(97 92 02 1) ISBN 92-64-13610-X   FF95   £13.50   US$24.00   DM40

Reforming Agricultural Policies : Quantitative Restrictions on Production. Direct Income Support (1990)
(51 90 06 1) ISBN 92-64-13414-X   FF115   £14.00   US$24.00   DM45

Water Resource Management : Integrated Policies (1989)
(97 89 05 1) ISBN 92-64-13285-6   FF110   £13.50   US$24.00   DM46

Prices charged at the OECD Bookshop.

THE OECD CATALOGUE OF PUBLICATIONS and supplements will be sent free of charge on request addressed either to OECD Publications Service, or to the OECD Distributor in your country.

Table of Contents

Executive Summary

Introduction

The interdependance between agriculture and the environment is becoming more apparent. First, an increased awareness of the environmental relevance of agriculture has emerged over the last decade from a growing concern about the consequences of some agricultural practices and policies that indirectly encourage negative environmental impacts. This may include: pollution of surface- and ground-water resources, soil erosion and compaction, drainage of wetlands, air pollution, reduction or loss of species habitat diversity, and clearance of marginal agricultural land. Policies which provide commodity specific price and income supports can insulate the producers from market signals and may also have environmental implications, such as encouraging greater intensity of land and other agricultural input use, disruption of the ecological balance and loss of public goods such as countryside amenity (OECD, 1991a).

Second, a reduction in environmental quality caused by non-agricultural activities has a negative impact on the agriculture sector and the productivity of the land base. This includes air and water pollution generated by industry and urban developments, wastewater disposal, global threats such as depletion of the ozone layer and climate change, as well as the discharge of heavy metal and toxic substances.

Environmental concerns in agriculture can partly be addressed by policy reforms that are focused on market orientation and reduced agricultural assistance. Since 1987 OECD Ministers have affirmed their commitment to a progressive and concerted reduction in agricultural support within a move towards greater market orientation. This was most recently confirmed in the 1991 Ministerial Communiqué. There was agreement that reform should, to the extent possible, simultaneously enable progress to be made on trade liberalisation and environmental objectives. Ministers also noted that environmental policies should be integrated more closely so that agriculture is carried out on an environmentally more sustainable basis. Progress in achieving reform has been very limited, however.

The focus of this study has been on the environmental aspects of agricultural policies. Specifically, the goals of the study were:

- to review progress made by OECD countries since 1988 concerning the integration of agricultural and environment policies;
- to elaborate a set of general principles and relationships which could guide OECD countries in the transition to sustainable agriculture; and
- to present a conceptual framework that establishes directions and priorities for further study. This will generally signal the ''agenda of work'' that relates to and builds on this study.

Information was provided by OECD governments and has been synthesized by government officials and the Secretariat under major headings in the preparation of this report. Because governments were the prime source of information, the study was concerned largely with developments initiated or directly approved by national governments; initiatives at a regional, provincial or local level were evaluated only to a limited degree. Also, most independent initiatives taken by farmers or farming organisations were excluded from the analysis.

Agriculture and the environment

Agriculture has always been very closely associated with the environment. This association is reflected by the production of food and fibre, the habitation of the countryside helping to maintain the viability and diversity of rural communities, maintenance of the landscape and habitats, provision of tourism and recreational facilities and environmental protection.

Farmers have a crucial role in reinforcing this association, through their dual and complementary responsibilities as producers of high quality food and fibre products and as custodians of the countryside.

The 1989 OECD report, *"Agricultural and Environmental Policies: Opportunities for Integration,"* argued that better integration of agriculture and environment policies would provide mutual benefits and, where necessary, enable tradeoffs to be made between competing objectives. Since the completion of that study some progress has been made by OECD countries in implementing policy integration. New developments, which reinforce the need for such policy integration, include:

- the desire of OECD countries to make a transition to more sustainable agriculture, recognizing the association between long-term economic growth and environmental protection;
- the recognition that reform of agricultural policies should be linked with improved environmental outcomes in a fair and equitable manner for farmers and the wider community;
- progress in developing environmental indicators for the agriculture sector, linking trends in sectoral economic and environmental performance for policymakers; and
- the heightened interest in environmental aspects associated with agricultural trade reform as part of the GATT Uruguay Round negotiations.

Events since 1988 have indicated the desirability of identifying goals and principles which could further assist policy integration. While noting that there has been some progress made by OECD countries in implementing integration measures, nevertheless it is necessary to identify new directions and priorities if future effort is to be focused and productive.

Goals and principles for policy integration

The achievement of sustainability of the natural resource base has emerged as a central national and international environmental public policy goal. Sustainability of the resource base is critical because the agriculture sector relies heavily on the quality and

8

quantity of the natural resource base, the sector produces a wide array of positive environmental services and affects the quality of environmental resources used by the public. Sustainable agriculture involves four aspects: an on-going economically viable agricultural production system, maintenance or enhancement of the farm's natural resource base, maintenance or enhancement of other ecosystems affected by agricultural activities, and the provision of natural amenity and aesthetic qualities.

Three general and inter-related aspects of the sustainability *goal* can be identified:

- *Sustainability is about being fair to the future, or intergenerational welfare.* More specifically, the central goal is to maintain a certain environmental stock, or its equivalent, for current and future generations. For the individual farmer, intergenerational welfare is accounted for in the transfer of stewardship of environmental and other assets to others;
- *To achieve sustainability, the private and/or public decision processes must incorporate the "shadow" prices of environmental quantity and quality dimensions.* Shadow prices reflect the social opportunity costs of using resources (such as land, water and forests), whether traded in markets or allocated in some non-market manner; and
- *Conservation of non-substitutable, irreversible environmental assets (such as wetlands and natural ecosystems) is critical to a sustainable natural resource base.* "Non-substitutable" and "irreversible" imply two conditions – that there is no apparent substitute for the environmental asset and that once the existing resource stock is depleted beyond a critical level, regeneration is not possible.

While these broad goals are essential to a clear understanding of general policy directions, the articulation of more specific principles is necessary to develop programmes for integrating agricultural and environmental policies.

The following *principles* reflect the current state of policy formation to achieve integrated agricultural and environmental policies:

- *View rural countryside assets as a source of agricultural products and environmental services.* The rural environmental base or countryside provides a wide variety of goods and services to the public, including food, fibre, energy, wildlife habitat, natural amenity and aesthetic qualities, waste assimilative capacity, etc. The set of agricultural and environmental services and values of those services varies widely over countries and even over regions within countries. Furthermore, as OECD countries' populations expand and incomes grow, the set of services desired from the countryside is changing: essentially the social values of non-production services are growing relative to those for traditional food and fibre goods in some countries. Agricultural products and policies are viewed as only one component of the rural countryside forces affecting resource use. This orientation requires a shift from the view of agriculture focusing exclusively on the negative or positive externalities to the management of the countryside in favour of a broader set of social objectives, including environmental management. Such a view requires prior assessment, monitoring, and evaluation of agricultural, rural and environmental policies to promote the integration of all social objectives for the countryside and rural resource sustainability;

- *Promote comprehensive resource allocation and use efficiency by directly or indirectly including environmental shadow prices.* Historically the price of many natural resources has been set too low to reflect full cost; furthermore the social costs associated with consuming the resource may be unaccounted for. The underpricing of irrigation water supply is one example, the underpricing of timber is another. OECD countries have to date made limited use of natural and environmental resource pricing as a policy instrument. Despite the complexity of the task, any progress in the field of pricing will be a contribution to sustainable development.

  Possible instruments include, but are not limited to, taxes on agricultural chemicals and purchase of land rights for environmental purposes. Although the mechanisms for incorporating environmental shadow prices are often imperfect reflections of true social opportunity costs, a broader concept of resource use efficiency to include non-market environmental aspects is emerging;

- *Alter agricultural commodity programme provisions that cause input, and crop or livestock output distortions which result in environmental degradation.* While many OECD countries are incorporating environmental aspects in their agricultural programmes, these have rarely been introduced in the context of agricultural policy reform. In fact in many countries environmental provisions are sometimes additive to existing, economically distorting price and income support programmes. This reform is intended to encourage the increased use of market signals in guiding supply and demand. By lowering agricultural programme incentives farmers would generally use natural resources at a lower rate, thereby enhancing resource sustainability;

- *Encourage farmers to recognize that it is in their and society's interests to maintain and enhance the farm's environmental asset base.* Farmers have economic incentives to maintain and enhance the farm's environmental asset base when they expect to receive current or future benefits in excess of associated costs. Such decentralized, "bottom up" actions give greater responsibility and flexibility to the actual decision-makers on the ground: the farmers themselves. Farmers may also perceive net benefits associated with some environmental actions that avoid the need for government intervention and associated costs, encouraging individual, voluntary solutions rather than government programmes;

- *Promote pollution prevention over waste management.* Measures to avoid pollution are often more flexible and less costly than trying to clean up waste. There is also less likelihood of causing irreversible environmental damage with pollution prevention techniques. While the pollution prevention concept is widely endorsed, programme initiatives across OECD countries are not yet common;

- *Target specific environmental objectives rather than use broad agriculture-environmental initiatives.* Within the context of overall policy integration, some OECD countries are moving towards more specific natural resource management targeting. This includes specifying goals such as protecting water quality in certain areas and wetlands preservation;

- *Apply the polluter-pays principle.* While OECD countries have agreed to apply polluter pays mechanisms their application is the exception rather than the rule. There are, however, a growing number of potential polluter pays policies in many OECD countries; and

- *Create the administrative framework to promote integration.* At a national level co-ordination among ministries and departments is achieved through numerous mechanisms (*e.g.* inter-agency consultation procedures, formal inter-agency agreements, joint working parties or task forces). Current administrative arrangements often ensure that environmental issues are considered in agricultural research. In these cases there is a strong interaction to identify the mutual influences and common paths to progress.

Some countries have re-defined and re-assigned responsibility for specified agricultural and environmental objectives to a specific agency. Others have established environmental units within agricultural ministries. Units with responsibility for rural affairs are also present in environmental departments. The incorporation of environmental aspects into economic decision-making at the earliest possible stage is strongly supported. There is a fundamental link between economic growth and the environment; policies cannot be made and implemented in isolation.

Progress in implementing policy integration: 1988-1990

i) *Policy framework*

In most OECD countries there has been a noticeable increase in the number of policies with an explicit or indirect environmental objective. Often such policies have been additional to existing agricultural price support policies. Environmental considerations are becoming an increasingly familiar element in structural policies particularly. The concepts of sustainable agriculture and sustainable development are receiving growing attention, confirming an increased emphasis on policy integration.

At the same time, developments in environmental policy have had a growing impact on agriculture in many OECD countries. In several countries, greater priority is being given to the control of non-point source pollution than in the past, often with clear implications for agriculture. At the same time established policies affecting land use, pesticide control, nature conservation, etc., are being extended or tightened and their impact on agriculture is therefore increasing.

The fundamental objectives of agricultural and rural development policies have been examined in several OECD countries over the last three years. Fresh objectives have included stronger commitments to integrate agricultural and environmental policies or the establishment of sustainable agriculture as a long run principle. National environmental plans or strategic documents which incorporate the agriculture sector are a notable new development.

Administrative arrangements vary greatly between countries and while environmental policy may be wholly within the control of an "environment ministry" in some countries, often responsibilities are divided and agricultural ministries not infrequently have responsibility for certain aspects of environmental policy, such as pesticides control and soil protection.

Institutional and procedural mechanisms for policy integration have continued to receive strong attention. In many OECD countries there have been changes in and re-definition of the responsibilities of the agriculture or environment ministries; in some cases wholly new agencies have been established. Inter-ministerial working groups, task forces, joint review groups and shared responsibility for implementation, regular review meetings and amended monitoring procedures are some of the administrative adjustments that have been made. This has been complemented by more extensive consultation procedures inside and outside of government to include farming organizations, NGOs, interest groups, indigenous people and community groups, as well as increased use of public hearings and inquiries and parliamentary review procedures. More extensive use of environmental assessment procedures and integrated land and water resource manage-ment approaches has also been evident.

A certain number of new environmental regulations have been introduced in the last three years and some of these have an impact on the agriculture sector. Many effectively impose constraints of some kind on farm practices; a few are intended to provide agriculture with protection from environmental damage originating in other sectors, for example the disposal of toxic waste on agricultural land. To be most effective, regulation needs to be dynamic to keep pace with evolving approaches to environmental protection. Only in a few cases has the polluter-pays principle been applied to agriculture.

New regulations tend to be focused on the use of pesticides, fertilizers, machinery and other inputs. Others concern undesirable outputs such as noise, waste products, odours, etc. Strengthened wildlife legislation and soil protection measures have also been introduced in a number of OECD countries.

ii)   Input measures

Two changes have been evident: the withdrawal or modification of some subsi-dies associated with environmental damage or resource depletion and, more significantly, the introduction of a range of new measures intended to promote more environmentally sensitive forms of agriculture (*e.g.* investment grants for waste storage facilities, pay-ments for soil conservation programmes, incentives to use reduced quantities of fertilizers or to adopt integrated pest management). However, while input subsidies may continue to be capitalized into land prices, this thus generates a double benefit to the recipient (through land capitalization and the availability of subsidies).

Many governments are encouraging the development and expansion of low input or organic farming partly, but not exclusively, for environmental reasons. Included in this category are production methods often labelled "alternative agriculture", "integrated agriculture", "sustainable agriculture", and various kinds of organic farming. Measures taken by governments include support for research, development and demonstration projects, the establishment of official standards and certification schemes, help in market-ing, advisory programmes for farmers and incentives to convert to organic forms of production.

A number of measures have been proposed or introduced which are intended to reduce or change the use of inputs in agriculture. The most commonly utilized measure is the withdrawal of agricultural land from production on either a temporary or permanent basis. Set aside of arable land is a policy employed in a growing number of OECD countries. Other measures include wider use of taxes on fertilizers, targeting of farm practices which may cause downstream environmental problems, tighter controls on and levies for pesticide use, strengthened procedures for pesticide registration and improved management of water resources through, for example, pricing to reflect the marginal social cost. Education, advisory and extension services are increasingly effective as are voluntary measures taken by farmers. The latter may be an element of a whole farm management plan.

iii) *Output and diversification measures*

There are relatively few cases where environmental objectives have had a significant influence on changes in the overall pattern of output subsidies. In some cases these subsidies have a clear environmental component but few of these have been of sufficient scale to alter the overall pattern of subsidization, which continues to be dominated by production related price and income support thus directed more towards production than resource conservation. The most commonly used policy measure designed to directly restrain output is marketing quotas. There is little evidence that quota systems have been amended in recent years to take more into account their environmental implications.

There has been a growing trend towards developing alternative forms of income for the agricultural community, sometimes with financial assistance from governments. These latter include measures to promote diversification of activities on farms such as tourist and recreation provision, crafts, small-scale food processing, afforestation, etc. and also employment off the farm. Some of these alternative sources of income are being developed irrespective of government action. Where agriculture is being maintained primarily or partly for social and environmental reasons, some diversification may be a high priority and may assist both the maintenance of current farming activities and improved access to and utilization of the farmed landscape by visitors and tourists.

iv) *External factors: international developments*

A number of developments at the international level are influencing the evolution of policy on agriculture and the environment in OECD countries. One of the most important concerns the debate on the reform of agricultural trade. Work in OECD has contributed to the analysis on alternative policy measures which would reduce trade distortion and which could lead to environmental benefits. GATT negotiations have led to an increased interest in "decoupled" forms of support for agriculture which are not linked to agricultural production, including payments to farmers which could be linked to the provision of environmental services.

International agreements on environmental issues are another influence on national policy development. Some of these agreements are at the international level, such as the 1991 Convention on the Protection of the Alps signed by Switzerland, France, Italy, Germany, Austria, Leichenstein and the EC; some are at the regional level, such as the International Conference on the Protection of the North Sea. A framework convention dealing with climate change was presented at the 1992 UN Conference on Environment and Development. Agriculture is both a contributor to and affected by potential climate change. First, as a source of or a sink for greenhouse gas emissions, agriculture could be affected by policies to limit climate change (*e.g.* reduction in carbon dioxide emissions through the development of forestry programmes, reductions in enteric methane emissions from crop or livestock production). Second, agriculture's capacity to produce food and fibre will be affected by the level and variability of climate conditions.

As noted in OECD (1991*a*) an important implication of production related price and income assistance, which continue to be dominant in the majority of OECD countries, may be increased environmental damage. This has resulted in greater intensity in the use of land and other inputs, leading to soil and water degradation, air pollution, loss of rural amenity and damage to ecosystems. Compatibility between environmental policies and sectoral economic policy should be a primary objective of policy makers.

v) *Outlook*

Progress in the direction of greater market orientation for agricultural production has been very limited; there are only two OECD countries, Australia and New Zealand, whose agricultural sectors respond predominantly to world market signals. Very few countries have taken measures to liberalise import access and indeed some have tightened existing restrictions.

The progress that has been made towards policy integration during the period 1988-1990 is a reflection of changing attitudes in this field, but it is still rather early to evaluate the impact. There is often a time lag between policy implementation and seeing the fruits of the new measure. In addition, many of the policy initiatives introduced have more than one objective and the extent to which specifically environmental goals have been achieved is not always clear. It would be unwise to place too much emphasis on the on-going changes or to exaggerate the extent of real integration that has been achieved. Further evaluation is required.

Overall, while there has been some progress over the last three years in incorporating the environmental aspects in agricultural policy, nevertheless in the majority of cases, environmentally related measures have been introduced in addition to, rather than as alternatives for, output related measures which have provided high levels of assistance to the agricultural sector. This often results in unresolved conflicts between agricultural and environmental policies, which highlight the need for integrated policies in this area.

A framework for advancing the integration of agricultural and environmental policy

Over the last five years several aspects of the relationship between agriculture and the environment have been directly and indirectly examined (OECD, 1986*a*; OECD, 1986*b*; OECD, 1987; OECD, 1989*a*; OECD, 1989*b*; OECD, 1990*a*). The range of measures introduced and those still required were identified and assessed for their efficacy, from the standpoint of both agricultural and environment interests.

While the studies have been systematic they have not covered in depth all aspects in both sectors. To place the context of future work within an overall strategy it is useful to set out an appropriate framework, recognizing that its application would have to be adapted to various situations of regions and countries.

i)   *Scope*

– Sustainable development is a common objective of both environment and agriculture policies; there are two distinct but complementary levels for the analysis. At the *policy level* this includes the issues of the design and implementation of agricultural and environmental policies with least economic distortions. This implies that policies are more market-oriented and that prices reflect the social value (externalities and public goods) of resources used;

At the *farm level* this includes issues of the environmental benefits of sustainable and lower input agriculture, the adoption of environmentally favourable technologies and practices, the role of education and farm advisory services, reinforcing the dual role of farmers as stake-holders involved in the use of more refined technologies and the production of safe products, and appeals to self interest.

For both levels the possible use of economic instruments, such as taxes, user charges, pollution charges and tradeable permits, should be examined. Such instruments can provide strong incentives to influence individual and sector behaviour and offer good prospects for achieving environmental objectives in a cost-efficient manner.

– As a first step, environmental policies should focus on the agricultural sector itself and identify the links with secondary industries related to agriculture, such as processing of agricultural products and the agricultural inputs supplying sector. This recognizes that secondary industries have an important relationship with the volume and quality of agricultural production. Detailed examination of those industries and their impact on the environment could be undertaken at a later stage; and

– The impacts of pollution on agriculture should be taken into account. These impacts include primarily air, water and soil pollution. The impact of urbanization, transport infrastructure, etc., taking up agricultural land, although having obvious environmental effects, has been addressed in previous OECD studies.

ii)   *Identifying new directions of work*

The Environment Committee Meeting at Ministerial Level held on 30th and 31st January 1991 noted that "Both environmental and agricultural goals should be pursued within the context of agricultural reform, the goal being to move rapidly toward 'environment friendlier', sustainable agricultural practices. There is particular need to introduce low-energy, low polluting systems based on new technologies; and prices for agricultural inputs that reflect more fully their environmental costs" (OECD, 1991*b*: 6). The 1987 OECD Council at Ministerial Level had agreed that environmental protection should be considered within the objective of agricultural policy reform. The 1991 Council at Ministerial Level indicated that "Agricultural reform, to the extent possible, should simultaneously advance trade liberalisation and environmental objectives. In doing so, steps should be taken to integrate agricultural and environmental policies more closely, so that agriculture is conducted on an environmentally more sustainable basis" (OECD, 1991*c*: 7).

More generally, the Environment Ministers "affirmed that a key to sustainable development, and thus to ensuring sound environmental management, lies in the full integration of economic and environmental policies" (OECD, 1991*b*: 5). Furthermore, they "underlined the need for governments to identify and eliminate those subsidies, taxes or other market interventions that distort the use of environmental resources, thereby impacting adversely on environmental policy objectives" (OECD, 1991*b*: 6). "Getting the price right" for raw materials, goods and services to better reflect their full environmental and social costs was seen as critical in this respect. The use of economic instruments to achieve environmental objectives in a cost-efficient manner was strongly supported.

Future work needs to be co-ordinated and focused within a framework of action. A number of new directions, which are not mutually exclusive, can be identified as:

- environmental components and impacts of agricultural policies;
- agricultural components and impacts of environment policies;
- external environmental impacts on agriculture; and
- the inter-relationship between agricultural, environmental and trade policies.

Environmental components and impacts of agricultural policies

Five key points can be noted under this heading:

- market prices for agricultural inputs need to be established (*e.g.* removing explicit subsidies for some forms of fertilizers, applying the polluter-pays principle, enhanced transparency in pricing of water, etc.);
- market prices for outputs need to be established (*e.g.*removing production distorting and trade distorting measures);
- further effort is needed to improve the integration of research, education and extension services together with programmes to influence farmer adoption of environmentally favourable technology and practices. The use of "bottom up", farmer-led initiatives is one means of implementation;
- the criteria for non-agricultural services should be defined, including types of services covered, definitions of "rural amenity", "landscape maintenance", etc. In addition, criteria for the pricing of environmental goods provided by agriculture should be established and to the extent that they are public goods, these should be valued so as to be independent of production; and
- the adjustment costs, environmental implications and production impacts of moving to sustainable and lower input agriculture should be addressed. The objective should be that such a transition be facilitated by non-production distorting measures.

The Committee for Agriculture is currently extending its policy analysis of agricultural policy reform, including the role of direct income support for farmers. The agriculture - environment relationship is one of four areas being considered, with reports on these areas now in preparation. The report on the provision of public goods will attempt to provide policy makers with a conceptual framework for the analysis of externalities and public goods and, eventually, an evaluation of current OECD policies of relevance to these areas against a set of agreed criteria. Within the context of the likely impact of agricultural policy reform on the level of externalities and the supply of public goods by agriculture, the report aims at assessing the appropriateness of direct income support and other means in this area.

Agricultural components and impacts of environment policies

All OECD countries have established wide ranging environmental policies and implementation measures. Most of these policies have been designed for industrial or household pollution. More recently, in a few countries specific standards and measures have been implemented to counteract serious agricultural pollution. In some areas of environmental policy, however, the agricultural sector is subsidized for the cost of compliance; for example in the case of manure disposal regulations, the Polluter-Pays Principle (PPP) is not always being applied.

In the field of resource conservation OECD policies are still relatively weak and agriculture is sometimes being exempted from them, *e.g.* water pricing. In some cases governmental policies are clearly contradictory and counter-productive to conservation, *e.g.* preservation of wetlands and extension of agricultural production and subsidized drainage of wetlands.

External environmental impacts on agriculture

The potential impacts of air, water and soil *pollution* from industrial, urban and transport sources on agriculture have been established and in some cases (on a regional basis) assessed and evaluated in economic terms. Air pollution, especially its photochemical oxidant form, has economic efficiency consequences involving regional and time-specific losses of up to five per cent of the economic surpluses associated with the production of annual crops (Crocker *in* OECD, 1989a). Air and water pollutants cause damage through foliage injury, crop losses, soil changes, introduction of toxics to livestock and crops.

Research into the potential impact of *climate change* that could occur through the emission of greenhouse gases is on-going. The impacts could occur through rises in temperature directly and some loss of agricultural land in coastal areas. The impact through rises in temperature is likely to result in regional shifts in production of certain crops as well as changes in production patterns in any specific region. Measures to reduce the emissions of greenhouse gases and measures to reduce the impacts of possible climate change could affect agriculture; for example, reduced use of fossil fuels, forest tree plantation programmes, the possible role of soil as a carbon sink, enhancing the significance of soil conservation/protection measures, and reduction of emissions from agriculture. It is noted that the Intergovernmental Panel on Climate Change (IPCC) and FAO have reported on the potential impacts on agriculture of climate change.

The impacts of *natural disasters,* such as flood, hurricane, earthquake and drought, may be exacerbated by human use of the natural resource system (*e.g.* clearance of fragile land for farming may increase the run-off load during heavy rain, encouraging landslip and erosion as well as increasing sediment loads and turbidity in downstream water bodies). This relates to both existing use and re-use of hazard prone areas as well as new development in such areas.

The *conversion of agricultural and other rural land* for urban land use and infrastructure development is common. Such conversion requires an assessment of the strategic value placed on:

- maintaining the rural landscape and habitats or representative ecological areas/ species thereof;
- the tradeoffs between competing demands, such as highway development or power transmission line or railway line routing and agricultural activities; and
- the results of planning measures to protect prime agricultural land.

Inter-relationships between agricultural, environmental and trade policies

An OECD study is in progress examining the linkages between environment and trade. An aspect of this work involves evaluating the relationships between agricultural, environmental and trade policies. The environmental effects of trade policies vary greatly and are generally closely associated with the environmental impacts of other economic and social factors.

Most OECD countries have applied trade measures (tariffs, quotas, etc.) to protect domestic supply and agricultural incomes. This has caused, in some cases, a misallocation of agricultural resources and disincentives for the adoption of certain environmentally favourable technology and practices (eg. lower input of fertilizers and pesticides). Thus, in some countries agricultural production exceeds the natural carrying capacity of the environment, while in others natural resources suitable for farming or husbandry are underutilized.

Trade instruments are increasingly being used to achieve environmental objectives at the national and international levels. The most common trade instrument is complementary restrictions on imports and exports as counterparts to regulatory controls on domestic production and consumption. The effectiveness of using trade instruments to encourage good environmental practices in other countries or to counter unfair environmental practices may be questionable. Proposals to use trade measures independent of internal environmental measures but to promote external environmental objectives, such as sustainable resource use in other countries, are increasing. Trade measures may have a role to play in influencing the price of imports to more accurately reflect their resource or environmental costs.

Generally, environmental and trade interests co-incide so that the removal of barriers which cause trade distortions will also reduce environmental distortions. In some cases, however, the interests of trade liberalization and environmental protection diverge: some countries have noted that free trade may have negative environmental effects, for example in the area of road transport. The problem is to identify where these conflicts arise between trade liberalisation and environmental protection. For example, certain trade restrictive measures may be warranted to enhance the quality of the environment (*e.g.* trade restrictions to control flows of environmentally damaging goods, facilitate transition programmes, achieve specific environmental goals).

There appears to be scope for combining trade liberalisation with environmental protection. Achieving this outcome may be difficult. The study under way seeks to indicate a way forward to guide OECD country actions generally and in specific sectors. In respect of agricultural, environmental and trade policy integration the preliminary work now in progress will provide a clearer perspective of the key issues involved. This could provide an opportunity to undertake further analysis at a later date.

iii)   *Quantitative analysis*

Work is continuing on an evaluation of what quantitative analysis might be conducted of environmental issues. A preliminary assessment of alternative *empirical approaches* used to analyse the linkages between agriculture and the environment, the types of information generated and potential contribution to the policy debate has been completed.

A preliminary set of *environmental indicators* for agriculture, energy and transport has been developed to identify trends of environmental significance, types of environmental impacts arising and key economic factors related to environment/economy linkages. Criteria for developing indicators were proposed as policy relevance, analytical soundness and measurability/ implementation. Work is continuing in all three sectors (with forestry being a further sector examined) and will focus on the analytical and policy frameworks in which to interpret indicators, further specification of indicators and testing with available data.

Setting priorities

The above listing of new directions is extensive in both topic range and the detailed investigations required for each topic. In any case the analysis of the fundamental issues concerning the *integration of agricultural and environmental policies* and of the progress made has to continue. Such work would have as its overall objective the promotion of a market-oriented, sustainable agriculture. This work will have to identify and define the key interactions between agriculture and the environment.

In this context, setting priorities is essential. The following priorities are proposed to guide future work on agriculture and environment policy integration; the priorities are, of course, inter-related within an overall policy making framework.

- There is a clear need for improved and more precise *definitions* and consistent *terminology*. Clarification of the terms and definitions used in discussing agricultural and environmental policy integration would provide a common basis for dialogue, analysis and monitoring. This would include, for example, defining better the meaning of "rural amenity" and environmental "public goods", both positive and negative.
- Establishing a set of *criteria* against which country actions can be evaluated is a further task. The development of common criteria for policy evaluation and further assessment of instruments that encompass non-market objectives of agricultural activities would be an integral part of this effort. Such criteria would include those necessary to evaluate the costs and benefits of lower input agriculture, and would also take into account the work concerning the role, implementation and implications of direct income support programmes.
- A better analysis of the possible use of *economic policy instruments and direct regulations,* as well as their impact is also of importance. Such instruments include taxes, direct payments, user charges, pollution regulation, etc.
- Progress is being made in developing environmental *indicators* in response to the mandate given to OECD by the 1989 Paris World Economic Summit (Summit of the Arche). Analysis could be undertaken to determine how the indicators for the agriculture sector could be further developed and then

incorporated into the existing, or an adapted, reporting format prepared by OECD countries on the state and outlook of their agricultural sector (for example as part of the annual agricultural "Monitoring and Outlook" report, and as part of environmental policy reviews of OECD countries).

– Once the results of the work on the linkages between *trade and the environment* are available, consideration should be given to undertaking detailed analysis of the relationship between agriculture, environment and trade policies.

– Reviewing the findings of the OECD seminar on the status, implementation and prospects for wider adoption of *sustainable agriculture technology and practices.*

References

1. OECD (1986*a*), Water Pollution by Fertilizers and Pesticides, Paris.
2. OECD (1986*b*), Rural Public Management, Paris.
3. OECD (1987) , Pricing of Water Services, Paris.
4. OECD (1989*a*), Agricultural and Environmental Policies – Opportunities for Integration, Paris.
5. OECD (1989*b*), Water Resource Management – Integrated Policies, Paris.
6. OECD (1990*a*), Modelling the Effects of Agricultural Policies, Paris.
7. OECD (1990*b*), Reforming Agricultural Policies – Quantitative Restrictions on Production and Direct Income Support, Paris.
8. OECD (1991*a*), Agricultural Policies, Markets and Trade – Monitoring and Outlook, Paris.
9. OECD (1991*b*), Communiqué – Environment Committee Meeting at Ministerial Level. SG/Press (91)9, 31st January 1991, Paris.
10. OECD (1991*c*), Communiqué – OECD Council at Ministerial Level, 759th Session. 5th June 1991, Paris.

Chapter 1

Introduction

1.0.   Setting the scene: reform of agricultural policies

In most OECD countries, agricultural production is heavily subsidized. This insulates farm commodities from market signals and, associated with border measures, distorts trade. In addition, trade protection measures inhibit market access for products from developed and developing countries.

Since 1987 OECD Ministers have reaffirmed their commitment to a progressive and concerted reduction in agricultural support within a move towards greater market orientation. This was most recently confirmed in the 1991 OECD Council Ministerial Communiqué. There was agreement that reform should, to the extent possible, simultaneously enable progress to be made on trade liberalisation and environmental objectives.

Progress in achieving reform has been very limited, however. The 1991 report on agricultural policy trends and outlook in OECD countries confirmed this (see OECD, 1991a). After declines in 1988 and 1989, because of short term factors which caused world prices to rise, both assistance to producers, as measured by the Producer Subsidy Equivalent (PSE), and consumer transfers, as measured by the Consumer Subsidy Equivalent (CSE), increased in 1990. The total PSE was US$176 billion, while the total CSE was US$133 billion. Output related assistance accounted for more than three quarters of total assistance. Production support is the most trade distorting, the cost of which is principally borne by consumers and taxpayers through higher food prices. There is a general tendency for domestic market prices of supported products to rise since 1987. The total transfer to agricultural producers from taxpayers and consumers combined was estimated at US$299 billion in 1990, an increase of 12 per cent compared to 1989.

Medium term forecasts covering the period to 1995 indicate that exportable surpluses of all products in the OECD area will increase if present policies are continued. A significant proportion of the forecast surpluses will, as in the past, only be disposed of on international markets with the aid of increased export assistance.

One of the reasons why agricultural policy reform has not accelerated since 1987 is because policy makers in many countries adopt a short-term perspective on the issue (OECD, 1991a). One-off events, such as drought, have diverted the attention of policy makers away from the decisions necessary to implement fundamental reform while the underlying causes of distortions have remained intact. Reform cannot be repeatedly postponed, however, without severe economic consequences. In addition, environmental concerns, *inter alia,* should not be used as arguments to avoid reform. The structural nature of the underlying surpluses is such that they will re-emerge if reforms continue to be marginal. This already occurred in 1990 (OECD, 1991*a*).

The Uruguay Round of international trade negotiations is also a major consideration. The final result of the negotiations depends on progress in a number of areas, including agriculture. The effects on markets of the outcome of the Round will probably not be immediate (OECD, 1991a). Furthermore, agreements will likely provide for gradual application of measures to reduce support and protection; there will be a time lag while domestic farm policies are designed and implemented to reflect trade commitments.

Reform of agricultural policies in favour of greater market orientation and reduced assistance is likely to lead to both economic and environmental benefits. The potential economic gains of reform, for example, have been modelled using the WALRAS applied general equilibrium model to simulate a full multi-lateral removal of average 1987 - 1989 levels of agricultural support. The resulting average real income gain was about 1 per cent; this is "very significant against the benchmark of the share of agriculture in GDP which lies between 2 and 4 per cent for most OECD countries. The reform of agricultural policies could therefore make a significant contribution to medium term growth" (OECD, 1991*a*: 35).

1.1. Agriculture and the environment

Agriculture has always been very closely associated with the environment. This association is reflected by the production of food and fibre, the habitation of the countryside helping to maintain the viability and diversity of rural communities, maintenance of the landscape and habitats, provision of tourism and recreational facilities, and environmental protection.

Farmers have a crucial role in reinforcing this association, through their dual and complementary responsibilities as producers of high quality food and fibre products and as custodians of the countryside. Farmers ensure the continued economic viability of agricultural production, the stewardship of the natural resource base of the farm, the protection, maintenance or enhancement of other ecosystems influenced by agricultural activities, and the provision of natural amenity and aesthetic qualities. Sustainable agriculture involves farm practices and systems that are compatible with these roles.

The contribution of improved technology to farm practices and systems which promote sustainable agriculture is notable. The use of minimum tillage, whole farm planning, integrated pest management and organic farming are some of the technological alternatives offering both economic and environmental benefits.

Over the last decade there has been a growing concern about the consequences of some agricultural practices and policies that indirectly encourage negative environmental impacts. This may include: pollution of ground- and surface water resources through the infiltration and run-off of certain nitrogeneous and phosphate-based fertilizers and pesticides; soil erosion and compaction; drainage of wetlands; air pollution from intensive manure production and crop spraying; loss of landscape amenity and habitat diversity; and clearance of marginal agricultural land. Policies and practices which encourage inappropriate resource use likewise have environmental consequences: intensified land use to produce higher crop yields, increased applications of agro-chemicals, single cropping agriculture and loss of biodiversity. Agricultural policies and practices are interlinked and it is necessary to focus on both in considering actions to improve agricultural and environmental outcomes.

A number of external environmental factors have a negative impact on agriculture. These include the potential impacts of climate change on the agricultural sector; the effects of external policies to limit climate change; air, water and soil pollution from urban and industrial activities; natural disasters such as floods, hurricanes and drought; and conversion of land from rural to urban use or for infrastructure facilities (motorways, sewage treatment plants, water treatment plants, etc.).

1.2. Opportunities for integrating agricultural and environmental policies

The 1989 OECD report, *"Agricultural and Environmental Policies: Opportunities for Integration"*, argued that better integration of agriculture and environment policies would provide mutual benefits and, where necessary, enable conscious tradeoffs to be made between competing agricultural and environmental objectives.

The report noted further that an integrated approach requires environmental considerations to be taken fully into account at an early stage in the development and implementation of agricultural policies. Likewise, during the formulation and implementation of environmental policies full consideration must be given to the potential impacts on agricultural production, incomes and prices. This view is reflected in Figure 1, which illustrates the trilogy of interdependent factors:

- the need to enhance the positive contribution which agriculture can make to the environment;
- the need to reduce agricultural pollution; and
- the importance of adapting agricultural policies so that they take full account of the environment.

A number of existing and emerging opportunities for policy integration were presented. Policy responses may, of course, apply to both circumstances. Possible actions included:

- developing research and advisory programmes with a greater emphasis and broader consideration of environmental objectives;
- strengthening education and advisory services to help improve the use of agricultural inputs and modify agricultural practices to minimise environmental damage;
- encouraging or requiring farmers to prepare management plans using inputs and practices that will protect and enhance the environment;
- entering into management agreements and other arrangements with farmers to improve landscape amenity and nature conservation;
- removing barriers to the adoption of environmentally favourable practices by farmers;
- introducing charges on inputs (*e.g.* fertilizers) and also for the cost of advisory, research and other activities designed to prevent and control agricultural pollution;
- enforcing regulations more stringently;
- further harmonising the standards and procedures used in regulating the use of agricultural inputs, including food quality and labeling standards; and

Figure 1. **Opportunities for Integration**

Administrative integration

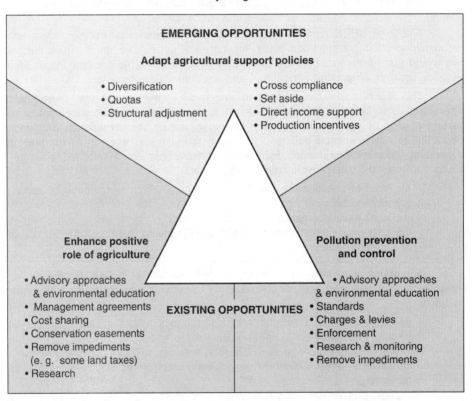

Source : Modified after OECD, 1989.

– making income, capital and land taxation policies neutral to agricultural and environmental objectives. This is in recognition of the potentially negative environmental outcomes associated with some tax incentives and concessions; such measures should not be used to directly influence environmental and agricultural objectives.

Emerging opportunities were identified as:

- the reduction of output-related support measures or the introduction of quantitative restrictions on production, which might result in decreased agricultural pollution;
- the provision and redirection of specific non-output related financial assistance to encourage farmers to continue with environmentally-favourable practices;
- changes to tariff arrangements;
- the introduction of cross-compliance requirements in existing land set-aside schemes;
- direct income support to farmers;
- the establishment of land set-aside programmes;
- the introduction of quotas on inputs and outputs; and
- setting aside highly productive land in filter strips along stream edges and in vulnerable groundwater areas.

All of the above could produce environmental benefits and budgetary savings from reduced surplus production.

1.2.1. Instruments for policy integration

The different approaches to the integration of agricultural and environmental policies are the institutional (administrative), procedural and policy instrument levels. Figure 2 summarises these approaches.

Environment Ministers of OECD countries, meeting in January 1991, identified agriculture as one sector in which improved policy integration and a consistent application of the Polluter-Pays Principle offer major returns (see OECD, 1991b). They noted that both environmental and agricultural goals should be pursued within the context of agricultural reform – the goal being to move rapidly toward "environment friendlier", sustainable agricultural practices. This view was reinforced by the OECD Council at Ministerial level which noted that environmental policies should be integrated more closely so that agriculture is carried out on an environmentally more sustainable basis (OECD, 1991c).

"Getting the prices right" for agricultural inputs and outputs to better reflect their full environmental and social costs is critical to successful policy integration. Market failure (e.g. non-payment or under-payment for resource depletion and damage) or intervention failure (e.g. under-supply of public goods) are notable impediments to assigning prices to raw materials, goods and services.

The use of economic instruments (e.g. taxes, charges) as a complement to regulatory instruments for environmental management is receiving greater attention. Economic instruments provide strong incentives for technological innovation and behavioural change and have the potential to achieve environmental objectives in a cost-efficient manner. Taxes on pesticides and fertilizers, already introduced in some OECD countries, are an example of this type of instrument (see Chapter 3).

Regulation continues to be an important instrument for policy-making. To be most effective it needs to be dynamic and keep pace with evolving approaches to environmental protection. Economic instruments and regulation can be used in a reinforcing manner to promote policy integration.

Figure 2. **Country Approaches to Integration**

ADMINISTRATIVE INTEGRATION

– National
  • Create an Environment Ministry
  • Assign joint responsibilities among relevant departments/ministries and promote co-ordination

– National and regional level
  • Create laws which require integration

INTEGRATION PROCEDURES

  • Change policy formulation process
  • Public participation
  • Inquiries, task forces and working groups
  • Land-use planning
  • Environmental impact assessment
  • Voluntary agreements

INTEGRATION INSTRUMENTS

– Advisory approaches
  • Direct advice to farmers
  • Education via media, etc. to farmers and general public
  • Farmer initiated conservation schemes
  • Consumer opinion and choice, "eco-labelling" of products
  • Environmental indicators

– Economic approaches
  • Input taxes
  • Implementation of the Polluter-Pays Principle
  • Land set-aside
  • Direct conservation payments
  • Removal of subsidies which encourage higher output and inappropriate resource use

– Regulatory approaches
  • Chemical standards (Fertilizers & Pesticides)
  • Restrictions on potentially polluting agricultural practices
  • Prohibition of undesirable agricultural practices
  • Licensing requirements

Modified after OECD, 1989.

1.3. The study

The period 1988-1990 has seen the proposal and introduction of agricultural and environmental policy initiatives that anticipate and respond to internal and external circumstances. This has been assisted by the desire of OECD countries to make a transition to more sustainable agriculture, recognising the association between long term economic growth and environmental protection; the recognition that reform in agricultural trade policies should be linked with improved environmental outcomes in a fair and equitable manner for farmers and the wider community; work on developing environmental indicators for agriculture which would assist policy formulation; and the heightened interest in environmental aspects associated with agricultural trade reform as part of the GATT Uruguay Round negotiations.

It is relevant to assess the state of progress OECD countries have made in terms of policies, instruments used, regulations, etc. Such an assessment not only enables the range of initiatives proposed or introduced to be evaluated and compared, but also provides an indication of the progress countries are making towards integration of agriculture and environment policies. It also allows new directions and priorities for further consolidating this integration to be identified.

1.3.1. Study goals

The goals of the study were:
1. to review progress made by OECD countries since 1988 concerning the integration of agriculture and environment policies;
2. to elaborate a set of general principles and relationships which could guide OECD countries in the transition to sustainable agriculture; and
3. to present a conceptual framework that establishes directions and priorities for further study. This framework will generally signal the "agenda of work" that relates to and builds on this study.

1.3.2. Methods and data collection

OECD governments were sent a questionnaire that sought information on a number of themes:
- measures proposed or introduced to improve administrative arrangements for integration;
- identifying problems, priorities for action and principles to guide policy integration;
- policy action on inputs, agricultural practices, products, capital structure and development, research and education/advisory services, monitoring of environmental impacts;
- emerging opportunities concerning production and income supports, encouragement of diversification and environmentally favourable practices, establishment of quota and set-aside restrictions;
- other issues, such as the impact on the environment of natural disasters, new technologies in use which enable savings or increased efficiency in resource use to be made and policy measures to reduce negative external effects on agriculture.

Responses were obtained from *Australia, Austria, Belgium, Canada, Denmark, Finland, France, Germany, Greece, Ireland, Italy, Japan, the Netherlands, New Zealand, Norway, Portugal, Sweden, Switzerland, Turkey, the United Kingdom, the United States and the EC.*

In addition a special case study from New Zealand provides insight into the short term and possible long term environmental effects of withdrawing agricultural support.

1.4.   Format of report

This chapter has briefly introduced the wider context of agricultural reform and then focused on identifying the links between agriculture and the environment, reviewing the opportunities for policy integration, and establishing the goals and methodology of this study. *Chapter 2* outlines general principles and linkages which contribute to agriculture and environment policy integration. *Chapter 3* critically reviews recent experiences of OECD countries, based on the questionnaire responses.

References

1. OECD (1989), Agricultural and Environmental Policies – Opportunities for Integration, Paris.
2. OECD (1991*a*), Agricultural Policies, Markets and Trade – Monitoring and Outlook, Paris.
3. OECD (1991*b*), Communiqué – Environment Committee Meeting at Ministerial Level. SG/Press(91)9, 31st January 1991, Paris.
4. OECD (1991*c*), Communiqué – Meeting of the Council of OECD at Ministerial Level. SG/Press(91)31, 5th June 1991, Paris.

Chapter 2

Policy Integration Concepts

2.0. Introduction

This chapter presents a theoretical basis for policy integration between agriculture and the environment. Goals and principles are identified, leading to a discussion of the environmental linkages of agriculture and finally an outline of approaches to harmonize policies.

2.1. *Goals and principles for managing the environment and agriculture*

2.1.1. *Goals*

Sustainability of the natural resource base has emerged as a central national and international environmental public policy goal (World Commission on Environment and Development, 1987). The application of sustainability criteria to agriculture is critical because agricultural production relies heavily on the quality and quantity of the natural resource base, and produces a wide array of positive environmental services and affects the quality of environmental resources used by the public. Sustainable agriculture involves four aspects: an ongoing economically viable agricultural production system, maintenance or enhancement of the farm's natural resource base, maintenance or enhancement of other ecosystems affected by agricultural activities, and the provision of natural amenity and aesthetic qualities.

Integration of agricultural and environmental policies requires a clear understanding of the fundamental concepts underlying sustainable development. While there are myriad definitions of sustainable development depending upon the problem and institutional context, three common precepts emerge (Pearce, 1989):

- *Sustainability is about being fair to the future, or intergenerational welfare.*
  More specifically, the central goal is to maintain a certain environmental stock, or its equivalent, for current and future generations. For the individual farmer, intergenerational welfare is accounted for in the transfer of stewardship of environmental and other assets to others. The sum of individual intergenerational decisions may be supplemented by collective actions. Implementing the sustainability concept at an aggregate collective level is of course most challenging, requiring consensus on how to define the relevant environmental stock, both in quantity and quality terms (*e.g.* use of environmental indicators), and to what extent non-environmental capital and technology can substitute for certain natural resources. Ultimately these broad social questions can only be

29

answered through political processes, though natural and social sciences can help illuminate the tradeoffs involved in such decisions;

– *To achieve sustainability, the private and/or public decision processes (accounting systems) must incorporate the "shadow" prices of environmental quantity and quality dimensions.* Shadow prices reflect the social opportunity costs of using the resources, whether traded in markets or allocated in some non-market manner (*e.g.* public leases for federal grazing lands). Examples of possible components of shadow prices include charges for reducing the stock of certain nonrenewable environmental resources, the value of using environmental resources for waste disposal and the aesthetic qualities of natural resources in production. These components are comprised of values by users and non-users (*e.g.* option values). Implementing real shadow pricing ensures that the resources are allocated to the use with highest value in the present or the future. Resource values (prices) are determined by the assignment of property rights in the resources, the degree of competition in private or public markets, and other features of the institutional context in which trading or exchange of resources takes place; and

– *Conservation of non-substitutable, irreversible environmental assets is critical to a sustainable natural resource base.* The terms "non-substitutable, irreversible" imply two conditions – that there is no apparent substitute, either natural or manufactured, for the environmental asset, (*e.g.* rare plant gene plasm), and that once the existing resource stock is depleted beyond a critical level, regeneration is not possible.

The three sustainability precepts described above are interrelated. Deciding how to be fair to the future implies the application of certain social values or prices to particular resources, and determines the level of conservation of irreversible environmental assets through those implied values. While these broad sustainability goals are essential to a clear understanding of general policy directions, the articulation of more specific principles is necessary to develop programmes for integrating agricultural and environmental policies.

2.1.2. Principles

Several patterns are emerging from OECD country policies to manage the environment related to agriculture. Since the concept of sustainable development is immature in practice, the principles stated below do not necessarily always link well to the precepts described above. The appropriate interpretation is that these principles reflect the current state of policy formation to achieve integrated agricultural and environmental policies. The order of presentation is from broader to narrower, more specific topics.

– *View rural countryside assets as a source of agricultural products and environmental services,* The rural environmental base or countryside provides a wide variety of goods and services to the public, including food, fiber, energy, wildlife habitat, natural amenity and aesthetic qualities, waste assimilative capacity and other aspects. Moreover, the set of agricultural and environmental services and values varies widely over countries, and even over regions within countries (Ervin and Tobey, 1990). Acceptance of these facts implies that both resource management issues and potential management policies will be "locally sensitive" or variable across regions. Modern agricultural production systems are also placing greater demands on rural environmental resources due to technology and scale pressures. Also, as OECD countries' populations expand and incomes grow, the set of services desired from the countryside is changing. In essence, the social values of non-production services are growing relative to those for traditional food and fiber goods in some countries. Partial evidence for this assertion is the growing array of agriculture-environmental programmes (reviewed in Chapter 3). An appropriate example includes programmes to preserve traditional production practices, such as hedgerows, which provide aesthetic and wildlife habitat values for the non-farm public. These positive environmental services have been provided in the past by agricultural producers, but changing public demands may necessitate greater amounts than would occur without public programmes.

In this perspective, agricultural products and policies are viewed as only one component of the rural countryside forces affecting resource use. The broad rural orientation requires a shift from the view of agriculture focusing exclusively on the negative or positive externalities to the management of the countryside in favour of a broader set of social objectives, including environmental management (Bromley and Hodge, 1990). Such a view requires prior assessment, monitoring and evaluation of agricultural, rural and environmental policies to promote the integration of all social objectives for the countryside and rural resource sustainability;

– *Promote comprehensive resource use efficiency by directly or indirectly including environmental shadow prices.* Historically the price of many natural resources has been set too low to reflect full cost; furthermore the social costs associated with consuming the resource may be unaccounted for. The underpricing of irrigation water is an example, encouraging overuse of water and often triggering adverse secondary environmental impacts (*e.g.* waterlogging). To date, OECD countries have made limited use of natural and environmental resource pricing as a policy instrument. Despite the complexity of the task, any progress in the field of pricing will be a contribution to sustainable development.

A variety of programme efforts are underway to incorporate environmental values into decisions about countryside resource use. Instruments include taxes on agricultural chemicals and purchase of land use rights for environmental purposes (*e.g.* wetlands preservation). OECD countries increasingly are undertaking programmes to reduce environmental damage caused by agriculture (*e.g.* erosion control), and to promote environmental benefits of agricultural practices. While the programmes or mechanisms for incorporating environmental shadow prices are often imperfect reflections of social opportunity costs, they nevertheless reflect a broader concept of resource use efficiency that includes non-market environmental aspects to help attain sustainable resource use patterns. Quantification of environmental shadow prices, especially the non-market components, is in cases constrained by data availability;

– *Alter agricultural commodity programme provisions that cause input and crop or livestock output distortions which result in environmental degradation.* Many OECD countries are seeking reform of their agricultural programmes for fiscal, marketing, and environmental reasons. The underlying principle is to cause farmers to use price signals reflecting market supply and demand conditions. Recent agricultural policy reform efforts by Australia and New Zealand are examples. Another case is the US decision to freeze commodity programme payment yields at 1985 levels, causing farmers to use market prices for input (*e.g.* fertilizer) decisions rather than higher programme support levels (Hertel *et al.*, 1990). By lowering agricultural programme incentives, farmers will generally use natural resources at a lower rate, thereby enhancing resource sustainability;

– *Encourage farmers to recognize that it is in their and society's interests to maintain and enhance the farm's environmental asset base.* Farmers have economic incentives to maintain and enhance the farm's environmental asset base when they expect to receive current or future benefits that exceed associated costs. Such decentralized individual actions are desirable because they reduce the need for environmental programme administrative costs and give greater responsibility and flexibility to the actual decision makers managing the resources. Examples of this "bottom-up" approach include erosion control actions on fragile soils, salinization reduction schemes in irrigated areas and use of crop rotations for fertilization or pest control purposes. These individual actions can be encouraged through the provision of information and community-based and farmer led advisory services explaining potential benefits and costs. Farmers may also perceive net benefits associated with some environmental actions that avoid the need for government intervention and associated costs, thereby ensuring individual, voluntary solutions rather than government programmes. Private actions may also depend on tenancy arrangements. Competitive and unrestricted conditions should apply to both landowner and tenant to promote the full incorporation of environmental benefits and costs in leases;

– *Promote pollution prevention over waste management.* Important supranational and national policy statements include the concept of pollution prevention. Two prominent examples are the European Community's Treaty of Rome and the US Environmental Protection Agency's pollution prevention policy statement. The logic is straightforward: measures to avoid pollution are often more flexible and less costly than trying to clean up waste. And, there is less likelihood of causing irreversible environmental damage with pollution prevention techniques. Changing management practices to avoid contamination of coastal estuaries is an appropriate example. While the pollution prevention concept is widely endorsed, broad programme initiatives across OECD countries are not yet common. Some noteworthy examples include taxes or fees coupled with research and extension education programmes in some Scandinavian countries to reduce pesticide and fertilizer use;

– *Target specific environmental objectives rather than use broad agriculture-environmental initiatives.* OECD country policies are generally evolving from broadly oriented environmental instruments to more specific natural resource management targets. Emergence of environmentally sensitive areas (ESA's) in EC country programmes typifies the trend. Recent redirection of the US Conservation Reserve Program (CRP) is also a good example. Initiated in 1985, the CRP was first used to retire cropland exceeding a minimum erosion potential criterion, subject to an acceptable bid. The original approach did indeed reduce erosion substantially, but at considerable government expense and lost production potential (Young and Osborn, 1990). In the 1990 US Food, Agriculture, Conservation and Trade Act (FACTA), the CRP is continued but is transformed to an instrument to achieve much more specific environmental goals, such as to protect vulnerable water quality areas and with less emphasis on broad erosion control. The likelihood of effectively addressing serious environmental sustainability problems within a given fiscal budget is enhanced under targeting;

– *Apply the polluter-pays principle.* OECD countries have agreed to apply polluter pays mechanisms to recoup government costs of programmes to prevent and reduce environmental damages caused by agriculture (OECD, 1989). Yet, examples of its application are the exception rather than the rule. The political decision to implement polluter pays programmes runs counter to traditional agriculture- environmental programmes in many developed countries. However, there are a growing number of potential polluter pays policies in many OECD countries (*e.g.* fees on fertilizers and pesticides). Revenues from the fee assessments are often used to fund research into sustainable agricultural systems; and

– *Create the administrative framework to promote integration.* At a national level co-ordination among ministries and departments is achieved through numerous mechanisms (*e.g.* inter-agency consultation procedures, formal inter-agency agreements, joint working parties or task forces).

Some countries have redefined and reassigned responsibility for specified agricultural and environmental objectives to a specific agency. Others have established environmental units within agricultural ministries. Units with responsibility for rural affairs are also present in environment departments.

Administrative arrangements often ensure that environmental issues are considered in agricultural research. In these cases, there is a strong interaction to identify the mutual influences and common paths to progress.

In some cases legislation and regulations concerned with land and water use have been amended to reflect an integrated approach to resource management. Agriculture, like forestry and mining, is one land use which has been subject to legislation with this emphasis in some OECD countries.

The use of environmental impact assessment and integrated land and water use planning are further administrative initiatives to promote integration. A key OECD objective is to incorporate environmental aspects into economic decision-making processes at the earliest possible stage. This reflects the 'fundamental link between economic growth and the environment; policies cannot be made and implemented in isolation. Continuous monitoring and evaluation are also required if policies are to remain relevant.

International co-operation is necessary to address transfrontier problems. Agricultural activities can cause or relieve transfrontier environmental issues; examples include sedimentation and chemical runoff to rivers and lakes that flow between countries, and air pollution impacts on crops and forestry production.

2.2. *The environmental linkages of agriculture*

The implementation of effective programmes based on the above principles depends critically upon a clear understanding of agriculture's links to the natural environment. Particularly important are the interactions of land and non-land resources defined by management decisions, and the influences exerted by agricultural and environmental policies.

Agriculture is linked physically to the natural environment through two fundamental processes. First, the *amount and type of land in production* reflects the *land extensiveness* of agricultural activities. As agricultural activities expand or contract, land enters or leaves production, usually changing the environmental services coming from the land. Salinity/acidity changes, vegetation loss, or soil erosion may ensue when new land is brought under cultivation. The drainage of wetlands to allow arable crop production is another example. In other instances adding land to agricultural production can improve desired environmental services, as in the case of reclaiming abandoned farmland to managed natural amenities in some European countries.

The second process captures the *amount and type of non-land inputs* that are combined with the land to produce crops and livestock. Increases in the amount of non-land inputs *per unit of land* are termed *input intensification.*[1] Much of the public concern about agriculture's environmental effects in OECD countries is centered on input intensification, especially the heightened use of agricultural chemicals. Leaching of nitrates to groundwater aquifers in the European Community and the US are prominent concerns. As with land extensiveness though, greater non-land input use does not uniformly cause environmental degradation. For example, when fertilizers and pesticides are applied in timely amounts and intervals, negative environmental affects can be minimized. Also, using labour and capital to build terraces for erosion control enhances environmental quality.

The total environmental pattern that emerges from agriculture's interaction with the countryside is the result of both land extensiveness and non-land input use. Consider, for example, the conversion of pasture grazing land to arable crop production. Cultivation of the former grassland will increase the potential for soil erosion and sediment-chemical runoff, but the degree of resulting water pollution depends on the types of cultivation and chemical use. As stressed above, these agriculture-environment interactions are quite sensitive to local conditions. For example, pasture conversion in Spain or Portugal may cause greater erosion than in northern Europe.

The processes of selecting land uses, applying non-land inputs to the land base and the resulting environmental effects can be broadly termed land management. A wide range of practices are available to the farmer that are consistent with sustainable development. Their use depends upon personal preferences and private and public economic incentives and costs. Within the land management concept falls the choice of particular technologies (*e.g.* chemicals) on certain soils and the decisions as to investment, timing and application equipment. Such decisions are critical to the environmental outcome, and capture the management dimension of agriculture. For example, mowing a meadow early in the year has a far greater impact on nesting birds than later in the year. Another example is dividing the total application of nitrogen fertilizer among seasons to avoid potential nitrate leaching.

2.2.1. *General relationships between agriculture and the environment*

The combined effects of land extensiveness, input use and management on the environment are variable over space and time, thus making any generalization difficult. Increased chemical use may not result in leaching problems in an area with impermeable subsoils for example. However, it is helpful to summarize the general relationships that underlie agriculture's interaction with the environment to build a framework for understanding potential policy impacts. The agriculture-environment process then depends on the spatial and temporal patterns of five factors in combination:

- crop and livestock production rates per unit area;
- amount of land in production (or rotation) of each crop and livestock enterprise, and amount of uncultivated land;
- environmental characteristics of the land resource (*e.g.* erodibility, leachability, precipitation patterns);
- amount of non-land input use per unit area (*e.g.* chemical intensity); and
- nature of non-land input use (*e.g.* chemical solubility).

The farmer's or rancher's decisions about combining these factors in the production process, termed the management dimension, then determines the set of environmental outcomes.

An illustrative example helps visualize how the factors may vary to give different agriculture-environment relationships. Consider two regions with distinctly different agricultures and environmental land bases. The first produces arable crops primarily, *e.g.* wheat, with pesticide intensive technologies on soils that are highly leachable with shallow aquifers. In the second region, a dairying/livestock grazing enterprise is practiced with animal manure fertilization on hilly land with high rates of precipitation and runoff. The two situations will likely produce two different time streams of environmental impacts: in the first case pesticide leaching to groundwater; and in the second case release of nutrients to surface waters. In addition, the nature of management in each situation can produce a range of different environmental outcomes with the same set of agriculture-environment factors.

A final dimension of the agriculture-environment relationship is the economic and social valuation of environmental services. Because of differences in relative resource endowments (*e.g.* land plentiful versus land scarce areas), social-cultural preferences or environmental conditions, different countries, and even different regions within countries, place substantially divergent values on similar environmental assets. A notable example is the preservation of hedgerows in some European countries which are not targeted in most US regions. The different values are expressions of varying environmental supply and demand conditions and help explain why environmental management programmes may differ considerably in various countries. The roles of environmental and social-cultural values in conjunction with the market and policy forces affecting agricultural production patterns are essential ingredients to understand in fostering the integration of environmental and agricultural policies.

2.2.2. *Agricultural and environmental policy roles*

Relative crop and livestock prices, input costs and available technology combine to determine agricultural production patterns in relation to natural resource conditions. It is through the price, cost and technology factors that agricultural and environmental policies influence the use of inputs and outputs in relation to the natural environment. For example, public programmes of advice and information for farmers in managing agricultural chemical use are intended to reduce information costs and thereby improve pesticide and fertilizer management efficiency. The price, cost, technology and policy influences depend upon the set of investments and agricultural structures (*e.g.* farm size and type) in the near term. In the long run, agricultural structures and the capital base also adjust to the market and policy forces. The discussion below explores the roles of different types of public policies that influence the use of inputs and output patterns. Following this, the opportunities for harmonizing agricultural and environmental policies are addressed.

Input subsidies

Subsidization of certain production factors encourages their enhanced use due to lower effective prices. A typical example of production-oriented subsidies is the provision of capital grants for draining wetlands or clearing woodlands for crop production.[2]

There are usually social goals for these input subsidies other than environmental quality, *e.g.* regional development. However, production input subsidies often have direct and indirect negative environmental effects, such as wildlife habitat destruction. In fewer cases, the subsidies are designed to effect environmental improvement, *e.g.* labour and materials cost sharing for planting tree shelterbelts.

OECD countries employ a wide range of measures to subsidize the use of specific inputs. In addition to land development grants, there are below-market water and grazing prices, soil conservation assistance, freight subsidies and crop insurance underwriting. Available data do not easily permit a full calculation of the share of total agricultural subsidies accounted for by input assistance. Reported estimates range from 0 to 15 per cent, with most countries falling in the lower end of the range (Webb *et al.*, 1990).

Lower production input costs exert two types of effects with potential environmental repercussions. First, unless all inputs are subsidized proportionately, the mix of production factors will vary from the combinations determined by market incentives. Credit subsidies may not materially distort the mix, but below-market input costs, whether they be for water, transport, grazing prices, etc., can cause environmental stress by encouraging excess use of resources and discouraging conservation and efficiency measures. The second effect is to lower the overall production costs of agricultural production, thereby inducing greater overall production on the natural resource base. Resultant environmental impacts of the production input subsidies depend on the spatial and temporal influences of the five determining factors discussed earlier (see section 2.2.1).

A smaller set of input subsidies is designed to remedy perceived environmental problems. There is a long history in some OECD countries of providing cost-sharing and technical assistance to increase the use of soil erosion control practices. The social efficacy of these programmes depends upon the degree of targeting to the most critical environmental problems and the extent to which subsidies match potential environmental benefits. Other examples include payments to establish wildlife habitat and irrigation efficiency improvements.

Land constraints

Rather than attempt to influence inputs indirectly through price, some public programmes attempt to control input use through direct constraints. The most notable example of a production input constraint is land set-aside for supply control. It comes in two forms: mandatory (usually in exchange for price and income support benefits); and voluntary (in exchange for compensatory payments). It can be exercised on a short term (*e.g.* annual) basis or for intermediate periods (*e.g.* five years). The effects of set-asides for supply control on the environment are complex. By artificially restricting land for crop production and raising its price, the substitution of non-land inputs, such as fertilizers and pesticides, are encouraged thereby increasing input intensity on the remaining production base (Offutt and Shoemaker, 1990). Set-aside land appears to receive minimal non-land inputs (*e.g.* for pest control) and thus may offset to some extent the increase in intensification on production acres. The net environmental effect of production set-asides depends on the individual country, region and period in question, as well as targeting for environmental objectives in its implementation (*i.e.* consideration of farm practices as a whole).

Environmental programmes also use land use constraints. The counterpart to production set-aside is long-term land retirement for conservation purposes. The Conservation Reserve Program in the US is the best example, with enrolment of approximately 34 million acres in 1990, and a scheduled goal of 40-45 million acres by 1995. Conservation purposes include erosion control, wetlands protection, water quality and wildlife habitat. Participating landowners receive compensatory payments and conservation cover establishment cost sharing in return for idling their lands over the 10 year contract period. As for other land constraint programmes, the conservation set-aside also induces input intensification on land remaining in production. Another example of land, use constraint for environmental purposes is the UK's environmentally sensitive areas (ESA's) management agreements. In return for payments to cover lost income, participating owners alter their land use and/or management practices to protect desired environmental assets. Finally, governments may restrict the development, leasing or use of public lands (*e.g.* wilderness areas, national parks or forests) for agricultural purposes to protect environmental ecosystems.

Output subsidies

OECD countries use a variety of programmes to support crop and livestock prices and farmer incomes. Deficiency payments, import levies, and export subsidies are some of the prominent approaches. Such subsidies exert at least four distinct forces with environmental implications (Miranowski *et al.*, in press; von Meyer, 1987):

- *Scale and intensity:* The subsidization of agriculture draws resources from non-agricultural sectors and encourages greater land use and non-land input intensification than would occur without subsidies. In both the US and EC, for example, intensification appears to be the dominant effect due to US set-aside and base acreage provisions and competition for agricultural land from non-agricultural sources in the EC;
- *Enterprise mix:* Differential support levels distort relative crop and livestock prices from world levels and may induce environmental stress through reduced production diversity. For example, higher US deficiency payments for maize than for cereals encourages greater maize production which usually causes more erosion and requires more chemical use than wheat, barley or oats. Similarly in the EC, the price support of maize and sugar beets compared to no support for root crops and dried pulses causes greater ecological risk (von Meyer, 1987);
- *Location:* The pattern of relative output subsidies creates incentives for higher spatial concentration of specific production types. The concentration may stem

from an area's natural productivity (yield) and/or input cost advantages for particular crops and livestock. Examples include cotton and rice production in the United States, and pig and poultry production near some EC port locations where imported feeds are relatively inexpensive; and

– *Technology:* The forces examined above reflect only near-term resource and output allocations. However, production subsidies also create dynamic effects through technological development and adoption (von Meyer, 1987; Schmitz, 1988). Price supports create higher incentives for research and development in those crops and livestock receiving the largest relative subsidies. Further, set-aside programmes create an artificial scarcity of land, thereby giving incentives for greater development and adoption of non-land input technology (*e.g.* chemicals). If the favoured crops and livestock create more environmental stress than less supported alternatives, the subsidies exacerbate environmental damages in the long run. This environmental pressure is in addition to the technological bias caused by the lack of effective input prices on non-market environmental resources.

Both public and private sectors supply new technologies for agriculture. The development of technologies promoting environmental values may have been neglected by both sectors in the past. Since little attempt has been made to assign market values to most environmental services, there is little private incentive for technology development to conserve the natural resources that generate these services. Indeed, there is ample incentive to promote technologies that fully exploit the ''free'' or low cost environmental resources. A below-market price for irrigation water is an appropriate example. These technology development incentives are most direct and strongest for the private sector but also extend through the public sector. Public education and extension programmes generally follow the pattern of emerging technologies and therefore may embody similar biases with respect to environmental values.

Environmental programmes can also use output subsidies to encourage greater production of crops and livestock that provide desired environmental services. Subsidization of grass and tree planting for environmental improvement (*e.g.* wildlife habitat, stream filter strips) are cases in point. However, since most crop and livestock enterprises can be produced in quite different ways that are either environmentally enhancing, benign, or degrading, there is only slight use of output subsidies for environmental purposes. Output subsidies for environmental objectives can of course change crop or livestock production levels, with implications for prices and trade. And, like all subsidies, tax revenues or other financial sources must be used which draw capital from other sectors of the economy. As noted above, it is the joint combination of inputs and outputs with natural resource conditions determined by management choice that produces the pattern of environmental services from agriculture.

Output quotas

Some OECD countries use marketing quotas to control agricultural supplies. The quotas have the economic advantage of allowing producers to organize their inputs in the most efficient manner compared to input constraints. Thus, output quotas do not generally induce the risk of distorting inputs and causing increased environmental stress (Reichelderfer, 1990). However, marketing quotas do not restrict land in production and therefore do not achieve possible soil and water conservation benefits due to set-asides.

A variant of an output quota is the marketing order which often employs size and cosmetic standards to control amounts sold in particular markets. By establishing differentiated markets, some control over market price is exerted. One potentially negative environmental consequence of the marketing orders which reward high cosmetic and size standards is the increased use of pesticides and chemical growth regulators to meet those standards.

Environmental regulations

Direct constraints (or regulations) are being increasingly applied to certain inputs thought to cause environmental degradation, such as fertilizer and pesticide applications, for water quality and food safety reasons. Virtually all OECD countries use pesticide registration programmes to screen out or restrict the use of certain compounds thought to cause human or animal health problems (OECD, 1989). Other regulatory measures vary widely to include pollution control efforts, such as restraints on straw burning and waste disposal, to nature conservation laws (*e.g.* protection of endangered species), to technology standards for buildings, machines and other practices to achieve broad environmental purposes. Also appropriate to this category are the charges or fees applied to agricultural inputs, such as chemicals, to alter their use or raise revenues for research into alternative technologies or public education programmes. In general, the effect of these environmental regulations is to constrain or shift non-land input use on the natural resource base to reduce environmental problems caused by agricultural activities. Given the rapidly evolving knowledge base about agriculture's environmental effects and acceptable pollution levels, the design of regulatory programmes should incorporate flexibility to accommodate dynamic circumstances.

Institutional forces

All of the policy categories discussed to this point bear directly on agricultural activities in relation to the environment. There are a group of policies and programmes that are less direct in their influence on the agriculture-environment outcomes. Examples include broad public environmental education efforts, product labeling requirements that promote better consumer food and fiber choices, and general environmental monitoring programmes that help define the scope and magnitude of potential problem areas. Finally, general monetary, fiscal, trade and technology policies can exert influences on agricultural prices, costs and technologies that feed back to overall environmental patterns of crop and livestock production.

Research, education and extension

All OECD countries have public programmes to develop agricultural technologies and to provide farmers with information and technical assistance for production, marketing and conservation purposes. The general intent of such programmes is to subsidize the development and dissemination of technology, information and management expertise. Because these programmes span all aspects of farm operation, their individual effects on production, marketing and environmental services are impossible to characterize here. It is sufficient to note that the programmes are mostly oriented to support perceived public needs in conventional agricultural production enterprises.

Research, education and extension activities can address current environmental problems in agriculture. Many topical environmental concerns require changes in management practices to alleviate the problem, such as the timing of nitrogen fertilizer applications. One approach to achieving such management practice shifts is to subsidize the research and development of technology and the provision of information and technical assistance to operators. Such services can be delivered in a voluntary fashion or mixed with regulation to help achieve environmental targets in a least cost manner. A programme of public research, development, and extension education will lessen the adjustment costs that the agriculture industry faces in meeting current and future environmental performance measures.

2.2.3. External factors

The integration of agricultural and environmental policies is subject to several important external influences. Perhaps the single largest potential force is international trade conditions and the market incentives that ensue. Not all environmental programmes are influenced by market price movements; for those programmes dependent on absolute and relative prices, and the variability of those prices, the achievement of environmental goals may be affected by price movements. The design of environmental programmes must recognize the important roles of world prices and their variability but the possible effects of price variability should not be arguments for production control and price stabilization policies.

Other important external factors include non-agricultural sector forces and global climate change. Urban expansion, infrastructure development and industrial pollution can affect agricultural land availability and the productivity of natural resources (e.g. the impact of acid rain deposition). The impact of natural disasters such as floods, hurricanes and drought also has short and frequently longer term impacts on agricultural productivity and land capability.

Agriculture has a dual role in global climate change and other environmental issues, such as acid precipitation. In respect of climate change, the first role is as a source of gas emissions or sequestration: agriculture could be affected by policies to limit climate change or acid depositions. Examples include reductions in methane emissions from crop or livestock production, reforestation for sequestering gases, and reductions in carbon fuel use for production activities. The second role recognises that agriculture's capacity to produce food and fiber will be affected by the level and variability of climate conditions, which will then define new spatial and temporal interactions with the natural resource base (Kane et al., 1991).

2.3. Approaches to harmonizing environmental and agricultural policies

The discussion of agricultural-environmental goals and principles and their linkage helps identify some basic steps or approaches for better achieving integration objectives. As with the preceding discussion, these approaches are general in nature but can serve to guide more specific programmes or policies.

i)   Reform production – related subsidies to encourage environmentally beneficial input or output substitution

Unless environmental objectives are incorporated in the design of production - related support, the production programmes will generally not promote social environmental goals, except by accident. There are now fiscal and international trade pressures to reform production subsidies.

A first step toward environmentally favourable reform is to divorce subsidies from specific crop and livestock enterprises and specific production levels. Although such action does not automatically guarantee a positive outcome for the environment, its implementation generates several environmental pluses: it reduces incentives for land conversion and non-land input intensification; it removes differential stress on different crop and livestock enterprises; it is likely to reduce the distortions in crop and livestock spatial concentration, and; it disconnects the forces pushing technological change toward subsidized crops and livestock.

Recent production programme reforms by New Zealand and Australia fall into this category. The US action to freeze programme payment crop yields divorces payments from actual production levels, but the crop subsidy programme continues to transfer capital from other economic sectors.

ii)   Design agricultural programmes to be complementary to desired environmental services

The first step is intended to remove the production subsidy forces causing environmental distortions. The next step recognizes that if support programmes decoupled from production are retained for other purposes (*e.g.* extension/advisory services), then their design and operation can help achieve increased levels of desired non-market/public goods environmental services. Implicit in this argument is the logic of cost effectiveness; if the public provides support to agricultural producers, then public goods and services, including environmental services, should be as high as possible for the tax expenditure. This rationale does not imply that such actions are the most cost effective or highest net benefit approach to achieving the desired environmental services.

Some actions have already been taken by OECD countries to tie agricultural programme benefits to environmental performance. The US environmental compliance measures are based on the principle that farmers must meet minimum environmental standards to retain eligibility for a broad array of production, finance and other subsidies. Similarly, the US Conservation Reserve Program makes subsidy payments to idle environmentally sensitive land which also contributes to supply control objectives.

iii)   Implement supplemental programmes for remaining environmental objectives

Reformed agricultural policies will not address all environmental problems related to agriculture for two reasons. Either the programme payments will be insufficient in amount or coverage to induce the desired level of response, or social preferences for certain environmental objectives are for approaches other than subsidies. In OECD (1989) two guidelines for developing supplemental environmental programmes were presented. First, for programmes designed to clean up agricultural pollution or to avoid environmental degradation, the polluter-pays principle (PPP) is to be invoked to cover necessary governmental expenditures. Application of this principle does not internalize all external costs associated with environmental externalities, but begins the process of changing price signals to farmers who cause environmental "bads". The second principle is to favor incentives or subsidies for the production of environmental "goods" or agriculture's positive environmental effects. Implementation of this policy approach (*i.e.* distinguishing between environmental bads and goods) requires the establishment of a reference point for judging degradation or improvement. For example, farmer actions to change water quality could be termed the avoidance of deterioration from a standard (and thereby subject to PPP), or improvement (and therefore eligible for subsidies) depending upon specification of the initial water quality standard set by public law; and

> *iv) Establish research, education and advisory programmes to complement environmental goals*

The transition from reforming production subsides that include environmental distortions to programmes fostering environmental improvement will necessitate adjustment costs. Public research, education and advisory programmes can lessen those adjustment costs through technology development and information dissemination. Moreover, those public programmes can be used to encourage farmers to undertake actions in their self-interest to maintain and enhance farm assets that are also complementary to social environmental objectives. Private industries have strong economic incentives to develop and sell technologies that are in high demand to reduce costs and/or increase profits. It should be noted that only if non-market environmental services are effectively priced or regulated will private incentives for technology development and distribution match social environmental objectives. The public sector research, education and advisory organisations do not face private market incentives but rather respond to governmental directives in response to political and bureaucratic preferences and decisions. While political and bureaucratic responses should conform to voter preferences in the longer term, short run adjustments will likely lag due to institutional constraints. A productive planning programme for research, education and advisory services can lessen the lags and ultimately deliver desired environmental services at lower public and private costs. In many OECD countries, public research and advisory programmes are already underway to encourage the development and adoption of environmentally favourable technology and farm practices.

Notes and References

1. The use of the term intensification is the opposite process referred to in the European Community as *extensification,* or the reduction in output (and thus inputs) per unit of land. That use of the extensification concept is different from the land extensiveness process referred to here, which does not incorporate an explicit measure of non-land input intensity.

2. Public expenditures for research, education and extension activities are technically subsidies to lower knowledge costs and promote improved productivity or environmental enhancement. Since these subsidies are not generally input specific, they are discussed separately.

Bromley, D. W. and I. Hodge (1990) "Private Property Rights and Presumptive Policy Entitlements: Reconsidering the Premises of Rural Policy." *Euro. R. Agri. Econ 17(2):* 197-214.

Commission of the European Communities. Treaty of Rome.

Ervin, D. E. and J. A. Tobey (1990). "European Agriculture and Environmental Policies: Sorting Through Incentives". American Enterprise Institute Conference – Is Environmental Quality Good for Business? Wash., D.C.

Hertel, T.; M. Tsigas, and P. Preckel (1990). "Unfreezing Program Payment Yields: Consequences and Alternatives." *Choices (2):* 32-33.

Kane, S.; J. Tobey, and J. Reilly (1991). "Climate Change: Economic Implications for World Agriculture", *Agriculture Economic Report, No. 647,* USDA Economic Research Service, Wash., D. C.

Miranowski, J. A.; J. Hrubovcak, and J. Sutton (in press). "The Effects of Commodity Programs on Resource Use," in R. Just and N. Bocksteal (eds.) *Commodity and Resource Policies in Agricultural Systems,* Springer Verlag.

OECD (1989). *Agricultural and Environmental Policies: Opportunities for Integration.* Organisation for Economic Co-operation and Development, Paris.

Offut, S. and R. Shoemaker (1990). "Agricultural Land, Technology and Farm Policy." *Jnl. Agric. Econ. 41(1):* 1-8.

Pearce, D. W. (1989). "An Economic Perspective on Sustainable Development." *Development 2(3):* 17-20.

Reichelderfer, K. H. (1990) "Environmental Effects of Farm Programs in Developed Countries." Presented paper. Sustainable Agriculture: Its Policy Effects on the Future of Canada and Ontario's Agrifood System. University of Guelph, Ontario.

Schmitz, A. (1988). "Issues in Commodity Trade: Implications for Natural Resources" in J. Sutton (ed) *Agricultural Trade and Natural Resources: Discovering the Critical Linkages.* Lynne Reiner Publishers.

US Environmental Protection Agency (1991). "US Environmental Protection Agency Pollution Prevention Strategy." Wash., D.C.

von Meyer, H. (1987) "Common Agricultural Policy and the Environment." Report to World Wildlife Fund International. London.

Webb, A. J.; M. Lopez, and R. Penn (1990). *Estimates of Producer and Consumer Subsidy Equivalents.* Statistical Bulletin No. 803. USDA Economic Research Service. Wash., D.C.

Weinshenck, G. (1990). "Strategies to Reduce Surplus Production and Environmental Burden". *Euro. R. Agri. Econ 17:* 215-230.

World Commission on Environment and Development (1987). *Our Common Future.* Oxford University Press.

Young, E. and C. T. Osborn (1990). "The Conservation Reserve Program: An Economic Assessment." *Agricultural Economics Report No. 626.* USDA Economic Research Service. Wash., D.C.

Chapter 3

Recent Experiences of OECD Countries – An Assessment

3.0. Introduction

This chapter is a review of agriculture-environment integration policies adopted in OECD countries during the period January 1988-October 1990. It covers a range of agricultural and environmental policies and attempts to identify areas where some measure of integration has been taking place. Information was gathered from governments by means of a questionnaire circulated by the OECD Secretariat. Information from this source has been supplemented by further material supplied by governments and a limited number of other sources such as the annual OECD reports on *"Agricultural Policies, Markets and Trade"*.

The main purpose of the survey is to describe progress in policy integration in OECD countries. It is not an attempt to provide an independent evaluation or to advocate a particular approach. In relatively few cases have governments themselves provided an evaluation of the outcome of policies recently put into place.

Since the survey is based on information from governments, it is concerned largely with developments initiated or directly approved by governments and refers to initiatives at a regional, provincial or local level only to a limited degree. Equally, it excludes most independent initiatives taken by farmers or farming organisations, although these have been significant in a number of countries.

Another consequence of relying primarily on a questionnaire of this kind is that some of the information provided is likely to be selective. For example, the responses cited very few examples of policy developments which have tended to increase pressure on the environment or to make integration between agricultural and environmental objectives more difficult. The review does not address the question of whether important opportunities for progress have been missed, for example by agricultural policy reform occurring more slowly than would have been possible. The questionnaire was not answered by every government and the amount of detail supplied was rather variable. Unavoidably, this introduced a further element of selectivity into the survey.

For these reasons, the survey incorporates some bias and this chapter paints an optimistic picture in the sense that it suggests more rapid progress towards policy integration and the solution of environmental problems than would be likely to emerge from a more independent exercise.

Since this review is concerned particularly with developments within a relatively short time period, it has not been possible to describe many policies in place prior to 1988. However, a brief account of policies adopted in earlier years is available in the OECD's 1989 report on *"Agricultural and Environmental Policies: Opportunities for Integration"*. Since October 1990, some countries have introduced significant new policies or have progressed with existing ones. Where details have been provided an account of these new developments is included in an annex to this chapter.

3.1. *Recent developments in agricultural and environmental policies: 1988-1990*

Adjustments have been taking place in agricultural policy in most OECD countries in the last three years, with many seeking to reduce the emphasis on market support mechanisms and the overall level of public subsidy to the sector. In most countries there has been a noticeable increase in the number of policies with an explicit or indirect environmental objective. Some of these policies have attempted to build an environmental component into measures with largely agricultural aims, others have addressed environmental problems such as soil erosion, or water pollution more directly. Environmental considerations are becoming an increasingly familiar element in structural policies particularly. The concepts of sustainable agriculture and sustainable development are receiving growing attention, confirming an increasing emphasis on policy integration.

At the same time, developments in environmental policy have had a growing impact on agriculture in many OECD countries. In several countries, greater priority is being given to the control of non-point source pollution than in the past, often with clear implications for agriculture. At the same time, well established policies affecting land use, pesticide control, nature conservation, etc. are being extended or tightened and their impact on agriculture is therefore increasing. Administrative arrangements vary greatly between countries and while environmental policy may be wholly within the control of an "environmental ministry" in some countries, often responsibilities are divided and agricultural ministries not infrequently have responsibility for certain aspects of environmental policy, such as pesticide control and soil protection.

For the purposes of this chapter the large variety of policies now in place in OECD countries have been divided into a number of principal categories and reflect largely those discussed in Chapter 2. In certain cases recent policies are discussed under more than one heading. The chapter concludes with some brief comments on the monitoring and evaluation of those policies now in place, on the role of external factors on policy development and the outlook for future policies.

3.2. *Policy objectives and principles*

Several OECD countries have been examining the fundamental objectives of agricultural and rural development policies in the last three years. In many cases fresh objectives have included stronger commitments to integrate agricultural and environmental policies or the establishment of sustainable agriculture as a long term principle. In addition, a number of countries have produced national environmental plans or strategic documents which include the agriculture sector. In most cases it is too early to judge the outcome of these strategic initiatives.

In *Canada* there has been a major redefinition of agricultural and environmental objectives with explicit regard to policy integration. A comprehensive review of the entire agri-food sector has been undertaken. Sustainability is one of the four main objectives (the others being market responsiveness; greater self reliance in the sector; and a recognition of national diversity). Federal and provincial Ministers of Agriculture have adopted a framework for action. On this foundation the federal government has formulated a policy on environmentally sustainable agriculture, with three objectives:

– to conserve and enhance the natural resources that agriculture uses and shares with other sectors;
– to be compatible with other environmental resources that are affected by agriculture; and
– to be proactive in protecting the agri-food sector from adverse environmental impacts arising externally.

The Canadian Green Plan proposes to support these objectives through long term programming aimed at promoting soil conservation, providing a clean water supply, integrating agriculture and wildlife objectives, managing waste and pollution, protecting genetic resources and addressing climate change and agriculture.

In the *US*, efforts to integrate agricultural and environmental policy go back at least to the Food Security Act of 1985. This Act created the ''sod buster'', conservation compliance and ''swampbuster'' provisions that made farm programme benefits contingent upon farmer conservation performance. ''Sod buster'' denies farm programme benefits to farmers who convert highly erodible land to cropland without approved conservation measures. It thus reduces the incentive to expand production on fragile lands primarily to receive government payments. Conservation compliance requires conservation on existing highly erodible cropland and ''swampbuster'' bars the conversion of wetlands to crop production. The Food, Agriculture, Conservation and Trade Act (FACTA) of 1990 takes this a step further by creating a new Agricultural Water Quality Protection Program which, with two other programmes, forms part of a more general Agricultural Resources Conservation Program designed to introduce more extensive environmental targeting into the US policy of removing land from production and minimizing any adverse effects from agricultural production.

In *Australia* sustainability of agriculture and integration of environmental/conservation and agricultural policies has been given high political support, with a commitment to sustainable development based on positive economic growth. A national strategy for sustainable development is being developed. Nine working groups have been established to consider individual economic sectors, including agriculture. A number of cross-sectoral issues, such as biodiversity, resource pricing and climate change are being examined also. In addition, a report on sustainable agriculture has recently been presented to the Australian Agricultural Council and its recommendations are being considered by Federal and State Governments.

A major review of the resource management legislation affecting land, water, air and minerals has been undertaken in *New Zealand*. The outcome is the Resource Management Act. Integrated and sustainable management of natural resources is a guiding principle and the emphasis is on creating a framework rather than a blueprint for resource management through focusing on environmental outcomes desired by the community.

New procedures in the Act for water management, soil protection, land use planning, hazardous substances and pollution and waste management will affect the agriculture sector.

The principle of sustainable agriculture has also received a great deal of attention in Europe. *The Netherlands* prepared two comprehensive policy proposals in 1989: a National Policy for Environmental Management and a Memorandum on Agricultural Structure; the latter sets out numerous measurable environmental objectives and proposes strategies for achieving them. The main farming organisation, the Landbouwschap, has also produced an Integrated Environmental Action Plan. The government's proposals emphasize the need for "planned change" and active adjustment.

The *UK* government recently issued an environmental strategy document entitled "This Common Inheritance", which is a comprehensive statement of government policy on the environment. With regard to the countryside, the aim is to preserve and, where possible, enhance the environment for the benefit of future generations. Policies which integrate environmental and agricultural objectives will continue to be developed and the government will seek to incorporate environmental considerations into the Common Agricultural Policy and other EC policies. While the document lists a large number of environmental objectives, many of these are qualitative rather than quantitative.

Some broad principles are being addressed in a proposed amendment to the *German* Federal Act on Nature Conservation. The assumption embodied in the original Act was that good agricultural and forestry practice serve the purposes of nature conservation and landscape preservation. By contrast, the amended Act will stipulate clearly that agriculture and forestry are expected to make a positive contribution towards the aims of nature conservation by considering ecological requirements when applying agrochemicals and gearing cultivation practices towards the conditions prevailing at individual sites.

At the same time new principles for compensation are proposed. In most circumstances compensation will be obligatory when nature conservation requirements result in economic costs for agricultural or forestry land uses.

In *Sweden,* agricultural and food policies have been the subject of far-reaching reforms. A new food policy was initiated by the Swedish Parliament in June 1990, based on the principle that agriculture should be subject to the same conditions as other sectors of the economy. This implies elimination of internal prices and market intervention, as well as export subsidies. The environmental goals of the policy include the preservation and development of a flourishing and varied rural landscape, and the reduction of environmental damage attributable to the use of agrochemicals and the leaching of plant materials.

In *Norway* the primary goals of policy on agriculture and the environment were set out by the government in two reports to the Storting (Parliament) in 1989. The first specified that the major goal is agricultural production which is in accordance with local natural conditions, "trying to minimize the loss of nutrients, soil and species, and to secure cultural and landscape qualities. The use of agricultural inputs must be adequate in relation to the standards of environmental and food qualities, their effects on the ecological systems, and a justifiable use of energy". Special consideration must be given to agriculture's role in maintaining populations and employment in rural areas.

The second document, which addresses the government's long term programme for 1990-1993, includes "Guidelines for Norwegian Environmental Policy". Amongst other things, these suggest that policy should seek a more varied land use, a better use of resources, the long term maintenance of the natural resource base for agriculture and the maintenance of a varied cultural landscape.

Other European countries are also developing environmental strategies. Examples include *France's* National Plan for the Environment and a major initiative combining water pollution and nature conservation, *Finland's* programme on agriculture and water protection and *Denmark's* proposed strategy for sustainable agriculture. Few countries have tried to define objectives as precisely as the Netherlands, however.

In the *EC* it is proposed to place a greater emphasis on rural development in future agricultural policy. The relief of environmental pressures is seen as a key priority for some of the most developed and intensively farmed areas of Europe. However, environmental objectives have also become more important in regions of less intensive agriculture, as reflected in the policy targets for the Ministry of Agriculture in *Greece* for example.

Integrated plans and programmes are usually confined to a particular set of problems, rather than the entire range of agriculture/environment problems. In recent years, water pollution has been the most frequent subject of such programmes, as in *Denmark* and *Ireland.*

3.3.   Input subsidies

Input subsidies cover a wide range of measures including direct subsidies intended to lower the price of immediate inputs to agriculture, such as water, and more indirect subsidies. An example of the latter is aid for research and development and farm advisory services, a subject considered separately in Section 3.11 of this chapter.

Until recently, most of these subsidies primarily were designed to increase farm productivity or output, with little or no priority being given to environmental objectives. However, many of these policies have been revised or recast in recent years resulting in a marked change in emphasis in many OECD countries. These changes reflect not only new environmental priorities but also budgetary concerns, attempts to control surplus production and several other factors. Very often the incorporation of environmental goals into the use of input subsidies has been perceived as helpful to or at least compatible with a reduced emphasis on increased production. Several governments are considering a further increase in the use of "decoupled payments", not least because of international pressure to reduce the scale of production-related support. The extent to which these payments affect farm incomes and production capacity often is unclear and is likely to require scrutiny.

In the period under review environmental integration with agricultural policies has been most evident in two forms:

– the withdrawal or modification of some input subsidies associated with environmental damage or resource depletion, continuing a previous trend; and
– the introduction of a range of new subsidies intended to promote more environmentally sensitive forms of agriculture.

Geographisches Institut
der Universität Kiel

3.3.1. Modifying established input subsidies

In a few cases subsidies which are of some environmental significance have been withdrawn, either for environmental or for other reasons. For example, in the *UK* investment aid for land drainage now is payable only in respect of replacement drainage systems following changes introduced under the Farm and Conservation Grant Scheme in 1989. In 1988 the *Australian* government decided to remove a subsidy on fertilizer use which had been in place since 1963. This decision was based more on a judgement that farm management practices had been improved than on a concern about environmental pollution, however.

Subsidies for *irrigation* are being modified in several countries. In *Australia* there has been a shift away from the historic under-pricing of water for irrigation purposes. Excessive use of water has led to salinisation, land degradation and reductions in river water quality. The principal responsibility for water resource management lies with the states, which have been supported by the Commonwealth in developing more appropriate and economically efficient water pricing and allocation policies. Progress has been variable, but many states have taken steps to reform pricing structures to take more account of the true cost of water supply. In addition, the issue of transferable property rights to the water resource has been under consideration. All States have introduced or are conducting trials of some form of transferable entitlement to water. Greater attention is being paid to the allocation of water supplies to their highest value uses. Nonetheless, there remains substantial scope for improvement and some states have advanced considerably further than others.

In *Canada* the concept of irrigation charges reflecting economic and environmental costs is new and not yet applied; use charges usually are minimal and favour agriculture over other uses. However, several provinces are beginning to take an interest in full cost water pricing. In *Japan,* however, irrigation subsidies are not regarded as environmentally undesirable and no salinisation problems have been detected despite the long history of continuous cultivation in many rice fields.

In *France* more realistic pricing of water for irrigation in some catchments has taken the form of a special charge imposed on farmers to take account of the environmental cost of over-use. In the Adour-Garonne catchment, for example, there has been an increase in this charge, which is imposed per hectare irrigated.

The *New Zealand* government's announcement in 1988 that it was to sell its shares in community irrigation schemes was a major change from the previous pattern of high levels of involvement in both the funding of scheme development and the management of the schemes on behalf of agricultural users. The principal reasons for the sales were to recapture a proportion of past expenditure and to allow more efficient pricing of irrigation and water services to occur. It is anticipated that water should now be priced at its marginal delivery costs, with a greater emphasis on conservation.

Investment aid, assistance for ''Less Favoured Areas'' and public support for land consolidation are amongst the considerable range of *agricultural structures* policies in place in European countries particularly. Several of these have been adjusted or reformed in order to introduce a greater element of environmental sensitivity. The role of these policies continues to be mixed. Several are designed to encourage structural changes, such as early retirement, farm enlargement and land consolidation, although such developments may be associated with adverse environmental change. Others are designed primarily to protect existing structures, for example by assisting the maintenance of a small family farm structure. Such policies may be justified partly or wholly on environmental grounds, especially where the maintenance of agricultural management is considered to yield substantial environmental benefits, as in Alpine regions for example. However, perceptions and definitions of environmental benefit vary between regions and countries and many policies address both social and environmental objectives without necessarily distinguishing precisely between them.

Some European Community (EC) policies have mixed agricultural, social and environmental objectives. An example is the 1975 Directive on less favoured areas which has been updated several times and recently has been amended, both to limit payments to larger farms and to allow Member States to vary subsidies to livestock producers in the light of local environmental requirements. Since the end of 1989 the subsidy, currently fixed at a maximum of 102 ECU per livestock unit, has been limited to 1.4 livestock units per hectare. This does not prevent farmers from carrying more livestock on their land but forms an upper limit on the subsidy. There are variations between EC Member States. In *Germany*, for instance, the limit is set at 1.0 livestock unit per hectare.

However, the EC limit permits a more intensive level of production than usually found in the less favoured areas. From an environmental point of view, the appropriate level of livestock density varies greatly from area to area and region to region; both over-grazing and under-grazing can cause environmental degradation. The need to respect local variations can reduce the value of setting standards at a national or EC level.

Most EC States have now incorporated environmental criteria into their structural policies and so modified the array of subsidies. For example, land consolidation and restructuring of farms continue to be encouraged in *France*, but environmental impact assessments have been required for larger schemes for several years and the inclusion of nature conservation areas is encouraged. Environmental impact assessments are now required for some of the other large agricultural investment projects which almost invariably are substantially subsidized. In *Germany* the Act on "Improving Agricultural Structures and Coastal Protection", which involves cooperation between the federal government and the Länder, was amended in 1988 to give greater priority to environmental aims and take more account of ecological requirements. Some potentially damaging forms of farm investment are no longer eligible for aid.

Another category of subsidy relates to the use of fuels in agriculture. In *Canada* fuel tax rebates and tax exemptions recently have been reduced as a budgetary cost saving measure. Less polluting fuels, such as natural gas, are being promoted, with grants for vehicle conversions.

In the *US* no new incentives to use less polluting fuels have been implemented since 1988. However, a $0.54 per gallon exemption from the Federal excise tax on gasoline is allowed on the sale of ten per cent ethanol/gasoline blended fuels. An alternative to the exemption is a Federal income tax credit equal to $0.54 per gallon of fuel ethanol produced or blended. The excise tax exemption and income tax credit reduce annual Federal revenues by about $500 million. In addition, States increasingly use direct payments to producers instead of state excise tax exemptions. Currently, only seven States allow unrestricted excise tax exemptions. State benefits average $0.15 per gallon.

Modifications to tax incentives or allowances available to agriculture have been the subject of review and policy initiatives in several OECD countries.

Land tax policies are being reviewed in *Australia* as a result of an acknowledgement that land degradation is a major problem. Assurances have been given that revised

51

taxation arrangements will be no less generous than those already in place. Amendments are intended to encourage practices which prevent land degradation as well as encouraging soil restoration.

Changes in the *US* income tax code in 1986 generally removed indirect incentives for conversion of wetlands and highly erodible range and pastureland to crop production. Incentives were reduced by restricting deductions for land clearing and drainage under soil and water conservation deductions, and eliminating favourable tax treatment of capital gains, including gains from increases in land values due to conversion. All States in the US use a preferential property tax assessment for agriculture, intended to encourage retention of land in agricultural production, etc.

3.3.2.   *New subsidies and incentive payments*

In the last three years there has been a considerable expansion in the number of aids for farmers which relate partly or wholly to environmental objectives. On the whole these are aimed at encouraging particular practices and forms of management, or stimulating diversification or new cropping patterns. Typically, they seek to lower the cost of desired investments or agricultural practices; many aim to subsidize labour or capital inputs rather than farm consumption of energy, fertilizers, agrochemicals, etc. In several countries expenditure on environmental schemes has risen substantially over the last three years. In *Norway,* for example, the budget for environmental measures was expected to rise from Nkr 450 million to Nkr 850 million in 1990.

Investment aids

Some of the new incentives are designed to encourage the adaptation of intensive systems in order to improve environmental management. One of the most common examples is the increasingly widespread availability in Europe of investment grants for livestock waste storage and handling systems. Capital grants for investments in slurry storage facilities typically are in the range of 25-50 per cent. In *Ireland*, capital grants are available for 55 per cent of the cost of constructing slurry and silage effluent stores and at 45 per cent for animal housing and fodder storage. In many cases such aids have been introduced or increased at the same time as regulatory standards have been tightened or other policies designed to influence farm practices have been initiated. In *Sweden,* for example, rules on farm manure storage capacity recently have been strengthened to require up to ten months of storage for pig and poultry wastes and eight months for cattle wastes. This change has been supported by a 20 per cent grant for enlarging present facilities. In *Norway* investment aid for improved manure storage, handling and silo facilities ranges between 30 and 50 per cent; with a limited budget, projects are ranked according to their likely cost effectiveness. The result is that support is directed primarily towards the extension of manure storage facilities in order to increase the length of the possible storage period.

Some of these investment aids have been introduced solely for a limited period, particularly where they are intended to ease a process of adjustment.

Others are expected to be available for a longer or, not infrequently, an indeterminate period. This raises immediate questions about their compatibility with the Polluter-Pays Principle.

One group of measures which have been introduced on an increasing scale in recent years is concerned with offering farmers payments in return for maintaining or altering certain management practices. Most of these payments are made on a regular basis, often annually, for a fixed period of time. However, some are in the form of a single once and for all payment, as with some easements in the *US* (in such cases a permanent transfer of property rights may be involved).

The nature and purpose of these payments varies considerably, but a large proportion have environmental objectives, such as reduced soil erosion, continued management of traditional landscapes, the maintenance or creation of wildlife habitats, the control of water pollution, etc. Many of the more recent schemes reflect a growing tendency towards offering payments to farmers for the provision of environmental services, sometimes associated with a willingness to compensate farmers for the effects of more stringent environmental regulations. Some of the main forms of subsidy are as follows:

- *tax incentives*. Reduced tax liabilities may be offered to farmers for complying with certain forms of management. Tax incentives are used by State and local governments in the *US,* where they play a role in some land use and conservation policies, providing an incentive to farmers and other landowners to agree easements, which may restrict their rights to develop farm land;
- *single, once and for all payments to landowners.* Usually associated with a significant transfer of property rights, for example forfeiting the right to alter substantially an area of wildlife habitat. Such payments are much less widespread than schemes involving payments on a regular basis;
- *compensatory payments.* Usually these are associated with a tightening of environmental regulations. In the *Netherlands* and *Germany,* for example, significant areas of farm land are designated as water protection zones within which restrictions on farming practice are compensated by annual payments per hectare affected. In many regions the area of such zones is growing while new restrictions on agricultural practices are being introduced. Policies designed to reduce the leaching of nitrates (and in some cases pesticides) into groundwater often restrict agricultural practice in the inner sections of these zones and may result in significant reductions in nitrogen fertilizer use, for example. Compensation scales generally reflect the extent of restrictions and their impact on farm incomes. Some of these compensatory payments take the form of multi-annual "management agreements". In the *UK* the level of compensation available in several forms of management agreement is based on the principle of profits foregone;
- *incentives for environmental management.* There are a growing number of policies involving payments to farmers or landowners for following specified forms of environmental management, ranging from set-aside (see Section 3.4.1) and soil conservation programmes through cultural landscape and wildlife habitat management schemes to incentives to use reduced quantities of inputs, such as fertilizers or to adopt integrated pest management. Many of these incentives could be described broadly as management agreements. The objectives of such schemes usually are either to ensure the continuation of practices which no longer appear economically attractive for farmers or to

encourage the adoption of new techniques such as integrated pest management or contour ploughing. Many schemes aim at maintaining environmental quality but a growing number have the objective of enhancing environmental standards. The level of payment usually is related to the cost to the farmer of the form of management required; very often this involves taking account of opportunity costs. *Switzerland* has been one of the first countries making extensive use of this approach. A variety of schemes involving contracts for farmers have been developed, with payments made in return for management practices designed to protect wildlife habitat and cultural landscapes;

– *incentives for low input and "alternative" forms of agriculture.* Several OECD countries recently have introduced schemes to encourage farmers to adopt low input systems, particularly organic farming methods. These incentives are rather different to those for adopting other forms of farm management in that they entail conversion to a substantially different system of agriculture with its own set of rules and the possibility of premium prices for products marketed. In several European countries, such as *Germany, Denmark, Sweden, Norway* and parts of *Switzerland,* farmers wishing to convert from orthodox to organic farming methods are eligible for special conversion grants to cover the period of changeover during which their income otherwise is likely to fall;

– *income support schemes based on payments per hectare,* with some linkage to land management requirements. Primarily these are designed to provide an increased income to farmers, for example following a cut in commodity support prices, but with some environmental benefits. At present such schemes are not common. *Norway* introduced such a scheme following signature of the Agricultural Agreement with farming organisations in 1989-90 and it has been reinforced subsequently. It applies to both grain and coarse fodder crops, with Nkr 1.3 billion being available for payments made on an area basis in 1990. Certain environmental conditions are attached to these payments, mostly concerning the protection of valued landscapes and wildlife habitat. For example, farmers have been prohibited from removing stone walls, ditches and paths and are required not to use pesticides close to semi-natural vegetation along field boundaries. Such policies require considerable monitoring and effective enforcement if they are to achieve their aims, and strengthening this aspect of the scheme is becoming a greater priority in *Norway*;

– *effects of pollution on agriculture.* These payments are relatively unusual but may occur when farmers are obliged to manage their holdings in a particular way as a result of significant pollution from other sectors. One of the most notable examples in recent years arose from the fire at the nuclear power station at Chernobyl and the resulting contamination of agricultural land and livestock with radioactive material. Compensation was paid to sheep farmers in the *UK* for restrictions imposed on the movement and marketing of stock. Larger areas were affected in *Norway* and *Sweden* where substantial programmes to limit health risks and assist farmers were implemented, aimed particularly at production of reindeer and sheep. Amongst the policies promoted strongly in 1987 and 1988 in *Norway* were measures to reduce the uptake of radioactive isotopes from the soil by vegetation and measures to control the intake by livestock of contaminated fodder. A government assessment of such policies in *Norway* suggested that they were effective in preventing dietary health risks and in maintaining consumer confidence.

With many OECD countries seeking to limit the output of agricultural products and to control expenditure on agricultural support, there has been a growing trend towards the promotion of alternative forms of income for the agricultural community. These include measures to promote diverse activities on farms, such as tourist and recreation provision, crafts, small-scale food processing, etc. and also employment off the farm. Environmental conditions may influence the targeting of such policies and the forms of diversification considered most appropriate in any given region. Where agriculture is being maintained primarily or partly for social and environmental reasons, some diversification may be a high priority and may assist both the maintenance of current farming activities and improved access to and utilization of the farmed landscape by visitors and tourists.

Diversification can be broadly divided into two types: diversification from "conventional" crops towards "alternative" crops, and diversification into non-agricultural income-earning activities.

In the *Netherlands,* the Ministry of Agriculture is carrying out market research for "alternative" crops which could have environmental benefits, such as flax. Other crops which are being considered in a number of EC countries include various energy crops such as short-rotation coppice. In *Sweden,* government incentives are available to farmers for planting energy crops, especially short-rotation coppice crops, such as salix species (willow). This is associated with the new food policy which includes the goal of abolishing internal market regulations. There are additional incentives for planting broad-leafed woodland and for the re-creation of wetlands. In *Austria* there are subsidies for producing a liquid fuel, "biodiesel", from rapeseed oil. One objective is to reduce the consumption of conventional diesel fuels in agriculture. *Finland* also is seriously studying "alternative" crops to provide raw materials for the pulp and paper industries as well as liquid fuels and lubricants.

Greece has emphasized the need for thorough research into the whole question of promoting new crops and new production methods by means of economic incentives. In particular there is a need to ensure that any such developments bring environmental benefits as well as responding to economic and market needs.

In general it is the production methods associated with new crops which will determine their immediate environmental impact. Where highly intensive management regimes are used, significant environmental costs may result.

In *Canada,* production-neutral income support programmes and reform of grain transportation policies are seen as two keys to diversification. Low farm incomes in the cereals sector are providing added incentives to diversify and these efforts are being spurred by research and promotion of new crops, longer rotations and stronger marketing efforts for non-traditional commodities. Inclusion of farm-fed grains and forages under the proposed new "Gross Revenue Insurance Plan" (GRIP) will reduce the incentive to sell grain for export, and provide an incentive to diversify into livestock.

In neither *Australia* nor *New Zealand* are there support arrangements for diversification; in the latter country there was a definite trend towards diversification between 1984 and 1988 to new livestock industries and horticulture. In the *US* there are three diversification schemes to encourage farmers to grow alternative crops. Legislative enactment is taking place in several States. Planting flexibility for supported crops has been introduced into the 1990 Food, Agriculture, Conservation and Trade Act (FACTA) to make production and input use decisions more responsive to the market. Under the 1990 FACTA, deficiency payments are now available for soil-building crops used as part of rotations. Lower support prices are also expected to encourage diversification.

Incentives to afforest agricultural land

i)   Objectives

One form of diversification which is being encouraged in several OECD countries is the afforestation of agricultural land. The objectives of such schemes vary. Some are aimed mainly at reducing agricultural output and removing land from production for 20 years or more. While it may be necessary to provide initial aid to establish new woods or forests and possibly further aid to supplement income during the years before harvesting begins, support costs may be lower than for surplus products, such as cereal crops. Budgetary saving is another objective of many schemes. In some countries there is an overall objective of raising the area of forest, either to increase timber production or for environmental and recreational purposes, or both. In a few countries, such as *Portugal,* soil surveys suggest that certain areas now used for agricultural production are not suitable for long term exploitation because of susceptibility to erosion for example, and reafforestation forms part of a land use strategy.

Most afforestation schemes have multiple objectives. While environmental factors usually play a part in the design of schemes, they are not necessarily of primary importance and some afforestation measures have led to considerable controversy and significant environmental damage. In most areas this is due to large scale planting of fast growing non-native species on inappropriate sites. The possible adverse affects may include soil erosion, soil acidification, susceptibility to fire, reduced water tables, destruction of wildlife habitats and traditional landscapes, etc. However, in several countries, environmental factors are an important influence on the design and execution of policies. For example, some governments are seeking to promote forestry as an aid to soil conservation and a more appropriate use of marginal agricultural land. Often forestry and agro-forestry policies are developed at a regional level and targeted at particular areas.

Most afforestation incentives will attract farmers on land which is agriculturally less productive and substantial incentives usually will be required to remove fertile soils from agricultural production. Such incentives are offered in few countries at present and the majority of afforestation can be expected to occur on soils which are marginal in agricultural terms.

ii)   Implementation

EC legislation is gradually extending to encourage afforestation, although forestry policy has been largely the preserve of the Member States in the past. In 1989 a number of new forestry measures were introduced, the most significant of which enables Member States to grant aid for the afforestation of farmland with financial contributions from *EC* funds. As with set-aside, governments have considerable discretion over implementation and rates of grant aid vary between Member States and sometimes between regions. *Ireland* has one of the lowest areas of forest cover in the Community and benefits from a high level of EC contributions towards afforestation grant aid as do *Greece, Portugal* and parts of *Italy, Spain* and *France.* In *Ireland,* forestry is seen as a major new land use and is strongly promoted to farmers. Private sector planting is estimated to have risen from 275 ha in 1981 to 11 000 ha in 1990.

There have been social or environmental conflicts or controversies over afforestation in several countries including *Ireland, Spain, Portugal* and the *UK*. Most stem from commercial afforestation policies involving fast growing species. In *Spain* and *Portugal* afforestation with eucalyptus species has been resisted strongly in some areas partly because of environmental concern. Environmental goals are important for policy in *Italy* for example, where the goals include nature conservation, landscape enhancement and the control of fires.

A significant feature of the new *EC* measure is that it follows precedents set by national schemes in paying farmers an annual sum to compensate for loss of income during the establishment phase of the new woodland (twenty years in the case of the *EC* Regulation). Farmers opting for afforestation under the set-aside scheme will also be able to benefit from this in future.

The *UK*'s Farm Woodland Scheme (FWS), adopted in 1988, incorporates this income-compensation approach. For both environmental and economic reasons the FWS, like schemes in several other countries, offers considerably higher payments for native broadleaved species than for conifers. However, take-up of this scheme has fallen well short of the target of 36 000 ha in three years. Additional schemes launched recently involve some government support for new "Community forests" on the outskirts of towns and a new "national forest" to be established partly on farmland in central England.

In several Scandinavian countries grant schemes are available to encourage afforestation with hardwoods. This is an important and well-established measure in *Finland* and also has been introduced in *Sweden*.

The control of erosion on agricultural land is a high priority in *Turkey*: 86 per cent of the land area is subject to water erosion and 65 per cent to wind erosion. In recent years 442 000 ha have been afforested as part of management efforts.

In *Canada* some provincial set-aside type programmes provide for tree planting on marginal agricultural land. Thus, in the Province of Prince Edward Island producers have an opportunity to plant marginal or sensitive land to trees through the Canada/PEI Forest Resource Development Agreement (1988-93). In the *US,* planting tree cover is one of the options under the Conservation Reserve Program. In *Japan* there is a policy to convert part of the current area of paddy fields into forest lands under the PFEP (Paddy Field Farming Establishment Programme). In *Australia* the National Afforestation Program was established in 1987-8, with the aim of helping to secure a resource base for the industry and reduce its reliance on native forests.

Two specific kinds of input subsidies concerned with farm practice merit particular mention since both grew in popularity in several OECD countries in the late 1980s. The two approaches are, respectively, management agreements and incentives for adopting low input or alternative farming systems. Each approach may contain several elements, including a mixture of subsidies and input constraints. They are considered separately here.

Management agreements generally take the form of a legal contract between public authorities and farmers (or foresters, etc.) whereby the latter receive regular payments or other incentives in return for providing specified environmental services. The nature of these services varies considerably and may include commitments to continue with existing systems, limitations on the use of certain inputs, restraints on specified forms of farm development or intensification, measures to enhance or maintain the landscape or ecological interest of a farm or a major change in the nature of production, *e.g.* from arable to grassland. Such agreements are often for a fixed number of years but may be indefinite. They may be associated with a written management plan or similar document. They are becoming increasingly common, particularly in northern European countries, where often they are instituted to support nature conservation or landscape protection goals, inside or outside protected areas. Such schemes may be operated by agricultural authorities or by a range of environmental or local agencies.

Until 1989, the management agreement approach was largely confined to the northern Member States of the EC (*Germany, UK* and the *Netherlands*). Under Article 19 of EC Regulation 797/85 (1985) governments were authorized to make payments to farmers within nationally designated areas in return for a commitment to adherence to environmentally sensitive farming practices. The EC contributes part of the cost of these payments under Regulation 1760/87, but initially they were adopted only by the three governments which already had experience with the use of management agreements. In some countries the costs and institutional and administrative demands of adopting this approach have inhibited new schemes. More recently however, there has been a growth in applications from countries such as *Denmark, France* and *Italy. Denmark* instituted a scheme in 1990. One per cent of the Danish agricultural area is expected to be covered by management agreements under this new scheme. *Ireland* also plans to establish a scheme of this kind.

In the *UK,* where the use of management agreements as a means of protecting sites of high conservation value has been established for some time, the principle of establishing Environmentally Sensitive Areas (ESAs) was initiated in 1987 and approved by the EC. The UK designated nine ESAs in that year with a further 10 in 1988/89, amounting to 790 000 ha in total. Within these areas, farmers have the option of participating in a five year management agreement with the Ministry of Agriculture in return for annual payments. The policy objectives within the ESAs are generally landscape and/or habitat protection, for example the maintenance of hay meadows and wetland grazing pastures. The scheme is being monitored and a first report on its operation was anticipated in 1991.

In *Germany,* the Länder are responsible for administering measures of this sort and a large number of schemes already have been established. Grassland extensification schemes are one example; these include requirements to refrain from pesticide spraying, reduce fertilizer use and leave meadows undisturbed during insect hatching periods. Other schemes operated by the Länder include those encouraging uncultivated strips along watercourses, strips along arable land on which farmers refrain from pesticide and/ or fertilizer use or cultivation in general, and appropriate meadow management for nesting birds.

France introduced an experimental use of Article 19 of Regulation 797/85 in 1989 in four areas and in 1990 decided to extend the programme substantially with the following four objectives:

- to maintain the landscape in areas where farming is in serious decline;
- to reintroduce winter and spring grazing in Mediterranean forests as a protection against fire;
- to encourage the use of green manure crops in winter in order to reduce leaching in areas of intensive cultivation with pollution problems; and
- to protect and conserve vulnerable habitats, especially wetlands.

So far fifteen areas have been designated, or await final confirmation under a recent initiative from the Ministry of Agriculture. More are anticipated, mostly with the objective of reducing nitrate leaching in areas of intensive cultivation.

The EC sets a limit on the scale of payment for management agreements which is eligible for partial reimbursement from the Community's agricultural budget. *Greece* is concerned that the level of reimbursement is not sufficient to control farming practices in sensitive wetlands (e. g. Ramsar sites). Voluntary management agreements will not be effective without higher compensation payments and restrictions will therefore need to be imposed instead.

In mid 1990 the EC Commission proposed amendments to Regulation 797/85 (now 2328/91) which would have made it obligatory for Member States to make management agreements available to all farmers. Under present arrangements, the implementation of Article 19 (now Articles 21-24) is optional for governments and is restricted to designated sensitive areas. Under these proposals, all EC farmers would have the option of receiving annual compensation payments in return for reducing their use of chemical inputs. However, by late 1990 these proposals had been amended and withdrawn and were due to be replaced with an alternative version in 1991.

In *Finland* a new law concerned with countryside protection has introduced the principle of management agreements. It is now possible to get government aid for a variety of different environmental purposes. Farmers wishing to participate draw up environmental plans which are evaluated by agricultural authorities. If accepted, these plans may lead to support payments of up to half the costs entailed. One of the first priorities is to improve the management of liquid manure.

Management agreements are also used in most other EFTA countries. In *Sweden,* for example, a budget of Skr 0.55 billion over a three year period has been allocated for a new programme whereby farmers will receive payments for the maintenance of open and varied agricultural landscapes.

In *Canada,* management agreements have been implemented under the National Soil Conservation Permanent Cover Program (NSCP) to secure the removal of highly erodible land from annual cultivation for periods of 10-21 years. Other agreements related to wildlife habitat are made under the auspices of the North American Waterfowl Management Plan. This Plan is funded primarily by private organisations, but supplemented by federal and provincial government funds. Under other agreements, producers have grouped together to implement Integrated Pest Management (IPM) with government technical and research support.

In the *US* management agreements of different kinds play a significant role in environmental protection. For example, the USDA and EPA have helped each state to develop water quality management plans. Eligible farmers will be invited to sign agreements of three to five years duration involving several obligations, including the implementation of an approved water quality protection plan. Cost sharing schemes with farmers are one variant of management agreements utilized in the US; one recent example is the USDA's experimental 1989 initiative for cost sharing with farmers adopting integrated crop management practices designed to reduce pesticide and/or fertilizer use. The Conservation Reserve Program (CRP) offering farmers payments in return for retiring land from production also depends on a form of management agreement. The CRP Program is described further in Section 3.4.1. The new wetland reserve programme will pay farmers to restore certain wetlands subject to a long term management plan. Conservation compliance and "sodbuster" require conformity to management plans in order to preserve a farmer's eligibility for farm programme payments.

A number of measures to encourage the protection of sensitive or important environmental features on farmland have been established or proposed in *New Zealand*. Protected areas can be set aside under four primary acts of Parliament. An indigenous forest protection policy for private and public land is proposed; a Forest Heritage Trust Fund for the preservation of indigenous forest with high ecological value is also proposed. Money for the Fund would be provided by the government to enable the purchase, lease or otherwise enable the protection of such forest as appropriate and agreed with the landowner. Heritage Orders to protect any place of special interest, character, value or visual appeal or of special significance to the indigenous people is a further measure being considered.

Encouragement of low input and organic farming

Both traditional and more recently developed production systems can fall within the broad category of "low input" agriculture. These include production methods often labelled "alternative agriculture", "integrated agriculture", "sustainable agriculture" and various kinds of organic farming, some of which have specialized rules of their own such as "biodynamic" agriculture. These systems may be based on traditional forms of production or on modified versions of contemporary agriculture but there is a common emphasis on lower inputs of inorganic fertilizers and agrochemicals and, in the case of organic farming, a central concern with the recycling of nutrients. Such systems often require special management skills and sometimes a greater input of labour than more conventional alternatives. Thus, they are "low input" in the sense that they are likely to involve a reduced consumption of off-farm inputs.

Many governments are now seeking to encourage the development and expansion of such forms of production partly, but not exclusively, for environmental reasons. The measures taken include support for research, development and demonstration projects, the establishment of official standards and certification systems, help in marketing, advisory programmes for farmers and incentives to convert from orthodox to organic forms of production. Other agricultural programmes, such as set-aside or "extensification", may also assist low input and organic farming, for example by providing support during a transition from conventional to organic production.

The degree to which existing agricultural practices are "intensive" or "extensive" varies greatly in OECD countries. Attitudes towards low-input and organic farming reflect this variation to some extent. In *Portugal,* where agriculture is mostly not intensive, there is little support for the promotion of low-input techniques. In *Denmark* a system of conversion incentives has been introduced to encourage those farmers interested in switching their entire holding to organic methods. The one-off payments range from 2 600 to 3 800 Dkr per hectare but a large take-up is not expected. In the *Netherlands,* where intensive production predominates, there is a considerable programme of research, development and promotion of low-input systems and organic agriculture is regarded as a strategic target towards which other types of farming might evolve. The government supports a number of experimental farms which are able to demonstrate economic and environmental advantages of low-input systems to other farmers.

In most other EC countries, official recognition of the value of low-input agriculture is relatively recent. In the last three years several governments have sought to clarify or establish new official standards of production. In *France,* the use of the term "biological agriculture" has been regulated since 1988 according to conditions laid down by independent organisations. The Ministry of Agriculture supports these organisations in advising and monitoring organic producers. A similar approach to setting standards for organic production and thus aiding marketing has been taken in several other European countries such as the *UK* where the demand for organic produce is growing. The EC recently has reached agreement on what will become a harmonized framework for regulating organic food production, concentrating on common rules for labelling, production methods and the monitoring of farmers to ensure that they are complying with the rules. A Community quality stamp will be introduced to signify the food which meets the EC standards.

The EC set-aside scheme is seen as having a potential role in helping farmers to convert to organic production. The great majority of farmers participating in the scheme are choosing the fallow option which could provide an opportunity to build up organic soil fertility.

The EC "extensification" scheme, introduced in 1988, also should lead to a reduction in the use of some inputs, such as fertilizers. This regulation initially was only experimental, requiring Member States to introduce pilot schemes, but now is a more permanent measure. Member States are to offer farmers incentives for "extensification" which entails reducing the output of specified crops or livestock products without any change in the land area involved. One variant entails farmers agreeing to reduce their output by at least 20 per cent within five years. This may be achieved by various means, including using a reduced level of inputs, notably fertilizers, or a lower number of animals. A second variant involves a five year agreement to convert the farm into a different form of production, such as organic farming. This "qualitative" alternative is intended to reduce output significantly. However, it is not necessary for each participating farm to reduce production by 20 per cent; the obligation is on Member States to demonstrate that the change in production methods generally will reduce output by at least 20 per cent. The only country to have implemented the extensification scheme on a significant scale is *Germany.* In 1989/90 2 100 farms signed agreements covering 48 000 hectares. The approach chosen has been the qualitative one, with farmers converting to organic production.

In *Sweden,* a three year programme of aid for farmers switching to organic farming was established in 1989/90, providing a grant of between 750 and 2 900 Skr per annum for the three years with the level depending on crop yields. This has been a success in that farmers have signed up a total of 30 000 hectares, compared with the present total of 10 000. In addition, nine government specialists are working with the extension services on organic farming and a special research and development programme has been set up by the Swedish Council for Forestry and Agricultural Research. In *Finland,* the National Board of Agriculture gave official directions concerning organic farming in January 1990 and there is also an active programme of research and system of subsidies for organisations providing advice to organic farmers. A transitional grant to encourage farmers switching to organic production was introduced in 1990. A similar grant scheme was introduced in *Norway* in 1985 offering transitional aid for up to three years. So far, take-up has been limited but it is thought likely to increase in future.

The promotion of integrated farming systems is also a priority in *Switzerland.* The Federal Government has been providing financial support for both research and advisory services to assist organic agriculture since 1990. Certain cantons also provide aid for farmers converting from orthodox to organic agriculture. A steering group has been set up to consider ways of promoting integrated farming systems. In *Austria*, a budget of Sch 38 million was made available for a new national scheme to encourage less intensive methods of production in 1990.

In *Canada* low input approaches, such as organic farming, have not been actively promoted although efforts are being made to develop standards for production, certification and labelling of organically grown commodities which should facilitate marketing.

In the *US* low input agriculture is not an explicit policy goal but there are proposals under the Sustainable Agriculture Farm Programme for increased voluntary use of traditional methods and diverse rotations which would still participate in commodity programme payments. In addition, a number of farmers' organisations have pursued low input sustainable agriculture initiatives, including pilot projects, conferences, and developing educational materials. At least 18 States have active legislation to provide for the certification of organic food, and legislation for a national system was included in the Food, Agriculture, Conservation and Trade Act of 1990.

There has been considerable interest in organic farming in *New Zealand*; this has been enhanced by promoting the ''clean, green'' image of the country's agricultural products. A computerized data base for organic production has been developed and an active research programme is in progress. This programme is studying systems under ''organic'' agriculture and horticulture as well as looking at systems where small inputs of artificial chemicals are made tactically rather than routinely. In *Australia,* there is no subsidy available for organic farming although the government is facilitating the development of appropriate standards and a certification scheme by bringing together relevant interest groups.

In *Japan* an organic farming office was established in 1989 for the study of the technical feasibility of organic methods and other issues. Consumer demand for organic products is increasing gradually but as yet there are no national standards; these are still decided by the individual producers.

3.4. *Input constraints*

The number of input constraints utilized in OECD countries is increasing. Government commitments to restrain or reduce output of certain commodities because of evolving environmental regulations which affect a range of inputs, such as fertilizers and pesticides, are an important reason for this change. There are distinctly different policy approaches in most countries.

3.4.1. Set-aside

The most commonly utilized measure for constraining inputs is the withdrawal of agricultural land from production on either a temporary or permanent basis. Set-aside of arable land is a policy employed in a growing number of OECD countries, particularly since the introduction of an EC scheme in 1988.

Policy developments and goals

The main purpose of set-aside policies, most of which are voluntary for farmers, is to control production, especially of cereal crops which are in surplus in many countries. Usually the total area set-aside is adjusted in order to meet market goals, although not all countries have formal targets for land set-aside.

The primary objectives of set-aside schemes generally are not environmental although some have been adapted to meet environmental as well as production objectives. Thus, environmental criteria are built in to several schemes and may affect either the land selected for set-aside or the form of management on the land which has been removed from production. In the *US* a firm link has been established between set-aside and the conservation of land with highly erodible soils.

In *Canada* environmental objectives are also central to the design of some set-aside programmes and there is provision for long term set-aside for up to 21 years, which offers greater scope for environmental management than the more common short-term schemes. In Europe, where soil erosion is less of a concern in most areas and set-aside schemes are more recent, environmental objectives tend to be more peripheral.

Policy implementation

The EC introduced a set-aside scheme in 1988, primarily as a production-control measure intended to complement reductions in market-support for arable products in surplus, principally cereals. Farmers who choose to participate in the scheme must agree to take at least 20 per cent of their crop-producing land out of production for a period of five years in return for an annual payment. The size of payment offered is determined by each government within limits set by the EC and may be subject to regional variations. Some governments, for example the *Netherlands* and *Germany,* provide compensation payments at the highest level allowed by the EC Regulation (600 ECU per ha.). In *Germany,* the level of payment varies according to the grade of soil, making the scheme an attractive proposition under a wide range of conditions and 223 000 ha were withdrawn from production in 1989/90, about a third of the EC total. In most other countries, take up of the scheme has been small; in *Spain,* where the payments offered are low, take-up has been minimal. Nor has there been much impact in *Ireland,* where the area of arable land is relatively small. Overall, less than two per cent of arable land had been taken out of production by 1990.

During the five-year period land set-aside may be either fallowed (permanently or in rotation), planted with trees or put to other non-agricultural uses. There is an obligation to establish plant cover on fallow land in order to reduce leaching of nutrients and to maintain good agronomic conditions. Mineral fertilizers and pesticides must not be applied. These obligations bring an element of pollution-prevention into the EC set-aside scheme and it is also possible but not obligatory to encourage nature and landscape conservation on land set-aside, as in *Germany* and the *UK*. There is also an option for EC

Member States to offer additional incentives for positive environmental improvement, although EC funds do not contribute to such payments. The *UK* has a "Countryside Premium Scheme" whereby additional payments are made to farmers who undertake practical conservation measures, such as restoring hedgerows and cultivating wild-flower meadows, in conjunction with set-aside. Approximately 3 600 ha of set-aside land were being managed under this scheme in early 1990, out of approximately 23 000 ha of potentially eligible set-aside land in the seven counties concerned.

The EC scheme has recently been amended, both to increase the level of payments offered to farmers and to allow Member States to encourage the production of certain "non-food" crops on set-aside land. In addition, the Commission proposed an amendment to the regulation in 1990 which would introduce an option whereby farmers could receive payments over an extended period of 20 years if they agreed to plant trees on the land. The environmental consequences of such changes in land use can be beneficial but may be detrimental, for example when inappropriate afforestation takes place or the production of "non-food" crops results in intensive cultivation and increased use of fertilizers and pesticides.

Sweden and *Austria* also operate set-aside policies for arable land (for periods of up to five years in the latter case). Others, such as *Finland,* encourage environmentally sensitive fallowing. In *Finland,* fallowing is obligatory: each farmer must fallow 15 per cent of the area of arable fields or pay a fine. There was a target of 350 000 hectares of fallow for 1991. The target has recently been increased for 1992. Part time farmers will be obliged to fallow between 20 and 30 per cent of their arable land in future, depending on the extent of their non-agricultural income.

As part of its National Soil Conservation Program, *Canada* has implemented a Permanent Cover Program designed to remove marginal or environmentally sensitive land from annual cultivation, for periods of up to 21 years. These programmes are voluntary and have been popular and successful in three provinces - Alberta, Saskatchewan and Ontario. The scheme is based on a bidding process whereby the applicant proposes a price per hectare which is assessed by a committee with the objective of retiring the most fragile land with the limited funds available. There are also a number of provincial programmes designed to restrict agricultural activities on lands bordering rivers and lakes. Some of these involve fencing off narrow strips of land, and planting trees to stabilize stream banks.

In the *US* the Conservation Reserve Program (CRP), established after 1985, provides the most significant environmental benefits from set-aside; farm owners or operators are paid to remove cropland from production for ten years. Currently 34 million acres are set-aside as grassland or tree cover, with the aim of reducing erosion, preserving soil productivity, improving water quality, and improving wildlife food and cover. At the end of 1990, arrangements for set-aside were amended significantly by the Food, Agriculture, Conservation and Trade Act. One of the principal changes was the re-targeting of the CRP to withdraw land from production where particular environmental benefits can be gained. For example, the CRP will be extended to vulnerable groundwater and surface water areas. A Wetlands Reserve Program (WRP) has also been established to restore wetlands from cropland. The new Environmental Conservation Acreage Reserve Program (ECARP) includes both the CRP and the new WRP. The Department of Agriculture is to enrol 40-45 million acres into ECARP by the end of 1995, including almost 34 million acres already involved in CRP.

In *Japan* there have been problems of rice over-production and a set-aside policy has existed for 20 years to withdraw land from rice production in favour of other crops (*e.g.* sunflowers). Farmers are being compensated and alternative crops are decided in relation to food production needs and rural landscape policies. In *Australia* producers of broad acre crops do not receive production-related subsidies and there are no quotas or set-aside provisions. Sugar production is subject to acreage controls and quotas but this is related to mill capacity, not environmental factors.

3.4.2. Other measures constraining agricultural land use

A variety of policies other than the planned set-aside or fallowing of agricultural land have the effect of constraining the use of land for farming purposes. These include:

- water pollution policies, which entail prohibiting or severely restricting agricultural activities in the vicinity of boreholes or sensitive water courses. In several countries including *France,* the *Netherlands* and *Germany* water protection zones have been established which may include small areas in which agriculture is prohibited or tightly regulated (see Section 3.4.4);
- land use policies, which affect the acceptability of certain agricultural practices in particular locations. For example, several countries have instituted regulations which prevent the establishment of intensive livestock units near to residential areas. The ploughing of grassland is not permitted in sensitive areas in several European countries; and
- some management agreements require farmers to remove small areas of their land from production in order to benefit wildlife, landscape features or public access to land (see also Section 3.3.2).

3.4.3. Taxes on fertilizers and other inputs

Most of the constraints on the use of inputs involve regulations or similar measures. However, in a few countries, especially in Europe, charges have been introduced on inputs, particularly fertilizers. Many of these charges were designed originally to reduce the quantity of surplus products requiring government support and to raise funds in order to finance government programmes in the agricultural sector, especially surplus disposal schemes. However, many of the schemes have been altered in recent years to include a more specific environmental element and in several countries the proceeds are now devoted, partly or wholly, to environmental projects.

In *Austria* there has been a levy on fertilizer use since 1986, introduced originally to help to control surplus production of arable crops and to generate revenues which have been redistributed within the agricultural sector. The rates of the levy were increased in August 1987 and are levied per kg of pure nutrient contained in inorganic fertilizers. Current rates are Sch 5 per kg of nitrogen, Sch 3 per kg of phosphate, and Sch 1.50 per kg of potassium. Consumption of fertilizers, especially K_2O, has declined subsequently but there are several reasons for this, including revised advice from the agricultural ministry, growing concern about the environmental consequences of high application rates, and a change in cropping patterns.

In *Finland,* where eutrophication of lakes and other waters is causing concern, a tax on phosphate fertilizers came into operation at the beginning of 1990. From the beginning of 1991 the rate was 1.0 Fmk per kg of phosphorus in the fertilizer, rising to

1.5 Fmk from 15 June 1991. The revenues collected are not being directed to projects concerned with agriculture's environmental role. This tax is in addition to a general fertilizer tax of 0.20 Fmk per kg which is used to help offset the cost of subsidizing exports.

Finland also has a tax of 2.5 per cent on the net selling price of pesticides, introduced in 1988. The revenues have been used to help finance the cost of maintaining the pesticide register and to offset the cost of handling registration applications. Several other OECD countries levy charges on pesticide companies to cover part of the cost of registration. A tax on the conversion of uncultivated land into agricultural use is also in force in order to discourage any further increases in the area of farmed lands.

In *Sweden,* as part of a range of measures, it is intended to reduce fertilizer consumption in order to reduce the volume of plant nutrients circulating in the agricultural system in the long run. The tax on both nitrogen and phosphate fertilizers was doubled in 1988 to reach 0.6 Skr/kg and 1.2 Skr/kg respectively, or about 10 per cent of the price. These are in addition to a 20 per cent levy on the price of fertilizers which is used to help finance the costs of surplus production. There is a proposal to convert part of this levy to an environmental tax when the price regulation ends as a consequence of the new food policy. Further increases in taxes will be considered if the target of a 20 per cent cut in consumption of nitrogen in fertilizers by the turn of the century seems unlikely to be reached.

Sweden also has a system of charges on pesticides with two components:
- a 20 per cent "price regulation" charge and associated levy of 46 Skr per hectare for each application of pesticides, the proceeds from which contribute to subsidies on grain and oilseed exports; and
- a 10 per cent environmental tax on the price of pesticides, the revenue from which is used to finance research, extension services and other elements of the programme for reducing pesticide risks.

In *Norway* there is currently a general tax of around 15 per cent on fertilizers. This tax rate has an important role in signalling the significance of the issue. Further increases in taxes will be considered in the future. In 1990 the revenues from this tax were redirected for environmental purposes, with 80 per cent being reallocated to farmers as an income support based on payments per hectare.

In the *Netherlands* there is a levy raised on surplus manure as defined by regulations which set maximum levels of phosphate which may be applied per hectare. In addition, a levy on pesticides is planned which will have the objective of raising 50 million guilders for use in pesticide-reduction action programmes.

The Flanders region of *Belgium* is planning to introduce an "environment tax" on the distributors of fertilizers and feedstuffs and on farmers who produce a manure surplus above the level laid down for their holding, although the central government does not consider this necessarily the best way forward. In *Denmark* the possibility of a fertilizer tax is also being discussed, following concern that the targets set for nutrient leaching from agriculture might not be met within the timetable laid down in the 1987 Aquatic Environment Action Plan. *Switzerland* is also amongst the countries where a tax on fertilizers has been proposed, mainly for environmental purposes.

In *France* there is a debate over the merits of imposing a system of pollution charges on farmers, notably for pollution by nitrates, in order to provide revenue for the water authorities responsible for pollution control. The farming organisations are opposed to the imposition of such charges *a priori*. The Ministry of Agriculture considers that it is essential to make a distinction between pollution from intensive livestock units and more diffuse sources of pollution from agricultural land. In the *UK* the Ministry of Agriculture believes that a nitrogen tax would have to be set at a high level to be effective in reducing fertilizer use, and would penalize the correct use of fertilizers virtually as much as their incorrect use. Nitrate leaching arising from incorrect timing of fertilizer application, from leaving land bare in the winter or from applying excessive manure in the autumn, would not be affected by a nitrogen tax. In the *US,* there is no national tax on fertilisers or pesticides. However, some States are levying taxes on certain agricultural chemicals on an increasing scale to reduce their use and fund research and environmental programmes. An example is the tax on nitrogen fertiliser in the State of Iowa.

3.4.4. *Constraints on the use of nutrients, including fertilizers and manure*

With growing concern about the prevalence of water pollution, potentially affecting both surface and ground waters, policies have been adopted in many countries in order to control the contamination of both fresh water and coastal waters. Some of these policies involve the preparation of national plans, as in *Denmark* and the *Netherlands,* which set targets for the entire country. In other cases, policies are directed more particularly at individual farm practices, such as the spreading of manure, or at especially sensitive areas, such as land overlying aquifers used for drinking water purposes.

Whereas the principal environmental concern about fertilizer and manure use in OECD countries is the possibility of water pollution, other concerns have also resulted in the introduction of regulations. One example concerns the heavy metal content of mineral fertilizers. In *Denmark,* recent regulations seek to prevent the sale of fertilizers containing cadmium above a specified limit. Similarly, there is concern about the content of heavy metals in sewage sludge. The application of sludge is regulated in most OECD countries and in many the standards are becoming more stringent, in some cases resulting in greater difficulties in disposing of sludge on agricultural land.

Some of the most extensive policies to control nutrient use in agriculture have been adopted in the Scandinavian countries and the *Netherlands* where there is concern about contamination of drinking water and about nutrient enrichment of fresh waters and marine waters. In parts of the Baltic Sea and North Sea, for example, there are significant eutrophication problems arising partly from nutrient run-off originating on agricultural land and partly from urban waste water systems.

In *Sweden* there is a programme which aims to reduce the leaching of nitrogen from agricultural land by 50 per cent by 1995 and to reduce phosphorus losses and ammonia discharges as well. One key measure is a system of controls over livestock density covering the whole of the country by a regulation which will come into force in 1995. From 1989, farms planning to expand or alter their livestock production must adjust to the new rules. These require that the supply of phosphorous in manure should correspond to the average needs of the crops during a crop rotation period, *i.e.* about 20 kilos per hectare per annum. This corresponds to about 1.5 dairy cattle or 10 fattening pigs a hectare. In making the necessary calculations, farmers can count in land which is grazed and also arable land owned by another farmer, provided that there is a long-term agreement to accept the manure. A few hundred farms are expected to meet difficulties in complying with this legislation and so will have to reduce their livestock numbers.

Other controls in *Sweden* include:

- A ban on manure spreading between 1 December and the end of February instituted in 1989, and additional controls on spreading in the southernmost parts of the country and along the coasts;
- Strengthened rules on manure storage capacity (up to 10 months for pigs and poultry and 8 months for cattle) supported by a temporary 20 per cent grant for enlarging present facilities;
- The institution of crop protection plans on all farms with more than 25 animal units, to complement manure and fertilizer plans. Farms must prepare all these plans by 1992, drawing on free help from extension officers if they wish;
- A plan to raise the proportion of arable land with "green cover" (either overwintering or catchcrops) from the present 40 per cent to 60 per cent by 1995; and
- fertilizer taxes (see Section 3.4.3).

Norway also has introduced regulations designed to reduce run-off of animal manure from agricultural land by setting a maximum limit on livestock density. Regulations agreed in 1989 set a limit of one livestock unit per 0.4 hectares of arable land on a farm. This must be complied with by 1995 or, in especially vulnerable areas, by 1993. No specific compensation is attached to this measure which also sets standards for animal manure storage facilities. There are complementary regulations limiting the time period during which it is permitted to spread slurry.

In *Finland,* the Council of State in 1988 agreed in principle a programme of controlling water pollution by agriculture, running to the year 1995. This contains specified targets, discussion of their realization and an estimate of costs. A joint committee of the agriculture and environment ministries is considering proposals for action. Current measures include strengthened controls over intensive livestock units, an information campaign by farmers, dairies and others on the collection of silage liquor, controls over manure application, subsidies for building manure stores in sensitive areas, selective loans for cowsheds and measures to reduce phosphate fertilizer use.

In *Austria,* a major amendment to the Federal Act on Water was passed by the Parliament in 1990, introducing the concept of "orderly agricultural practice". This legislation includes the establishment of upper limits on livestock density and the application of nitrogen fertilizers. If these limits are exceeded, farmers are required either to acquire a licence or proof that the relevant nutrients have been acquired in an authorized manner. Furthermore, threshold values have been set for organic and inorganic substances, including crop nutrients, likely to pollute groundwater.

The *Netherlands* has set a target that nitrate concentrations in groundwater beneath farmland should not exceed 50 mg/l at a depth of two metres below the water table in areas where groundwater can be used for the abstraction of drinking water. This target is to be achieved by the year 2000 by reducing the use of mineral and organic fertilizers according to rules to be laid down in 1991. (For surface water, the quality objective is already 50 mg/l.) One possibility is "minerals accounting", whereby the loss of minerals, whether from manure or inorganic fertilizer, would be controlled at a farm level. It is already used as an advisory method by the extension service. A study on the possibilities of using regulations and/or financial instruments for reducing nitrogen losses and pesticide use on farms is being undertaken.

Because of a heavy concentration of intensive livestock farms the problems associated with manure surpluses are high on the environmental and agricultural agendas. Targets have been set in the Memorandum on Agricultural Structures for reductions in emissions of ammonia and in the leaching and run-off of nitrates and phosphates. Measures to achieve these targets include limits on the amount of manure which may be applied to an area of land depending on the crop, the conservation value (in the case of grassland), etc. These limits will be reduced in stages up to the year 2 000, and should result in lower stocking densities. It is intended that measures needed to reduce pollution should be financed in part by the sector or enterprise involved. There is already a levy raised on producers of surplus manure, defined as more than 125 kg $P_2 O_5$ per hectare. A limited levy on mineral losses may be introduced in future.

In *Denmark*, implementation of the Aquatic Environment Action Plan of 1987 is underway. A major component of this is the obligation on farmers to meet standards for manure storage capacity, the control of run-off from farm stores and the level of application of manure on agricultural land. As in several other countries, the most burdensome obligation for farmers is the requirement to construct adequate manure storage facilities which are needed to avoid applications in inappropriate winter conditions. Under the original Action Plan, nine months of storage capacity was required. However, in 1988 this was modified to 6-9 months capacity on the approximately 25 000 farms with more than 31 livestock units, depending on an individual assessment of storage needs. This standard, which must be met by 1993, is more stringent than those in force in most other EC countries.

Some results of the Action Plan are now available, suggesting that more than half the livestock farms now fulfil government requirements for manure storage capacity and about 70 per cent of total arable land had vegetative cover in the autumn of 1989, more than meeting the official target. The overall target of a 50 per cent fall in nitrogen leaching by 1992 seems unlikely to be reached, however. The government was to present an action plan for sustainable development to Parliament before April 1991. One element is an effort to reduce the consumption of mineral fertilizers by increasing the utilization of animal manure.

The *German* Parliament has amended its federal Water Management Act to provide for the designation by the Länder of water protection areas where the use of agricultural inputs can be restricted or prohibited. Under these amendments the water authorities and/or water utilities must compensate farmers for any resulting income losses. Levies on down-stream water users are being considered as a means of financing such compensation. The *German* Environment Ministry is proposing a ban on the use of pesticides and fertilizers on strips of land alongside water bodies. This proposal is aimed particularly at tackling pollution along the North Sea and Baltic coasts. The Environment Ministry is increasing its budget for large-scale nature conservation projects by DM 10 million in order to finance projects alongside water bodies.

Together, the environment and agricultural ministries at Federal and Länder level have compiled a catalogue of "Agricultural Measures for the Avoidance of Inputs of Nutrients into Waters", covering a broad range of current and proposed measures, including reduced soil erosion, good agricultural practice, appropriate fertilizer application rates, the recycling of slurry, extensification and set-aside and the promotion of uncultivated strips along the edge of water bodies.

The Fertilizers Act has been amended to require that fertilizers are used only according to the principles of good practice and an ordinance on the use of fertilizers is being prepared to put these principles into effect. Guidelines for the construction and operation of manure stores are also being prepared. In addition, many of the Länder have developed their own ordinances for the application of slurry to avoid water pollution.

France has reaffirmed the value of its inter-ministerial committee on the reduction of nitrate pollution and is pursuing a strategy based mainly on research, advice and the promotion of good agricultural practice in areas vulnerable to leaching. Appropriate codes of practice for farmers are being prepared, such as the one prepared for legumes in 1989. However, it is foreseen that such codes may need to be supplemented by restrictions on farm practice. Some farmers are being encouraged to adopt nutrient balance plans, the most advanced being in Brittany where plans are obligatory for specialised livestock rearing units, particularly pig farms, over a certain size. The objective of protecting water supplies in areas of intensive cultivation is being included in the designation of sensitive areas under Article 19 of EC Regulation 797/85. Looking further ahead, a system of charges for nitrate pollution is being considered.

In *Italy* new legislation was introduced in May 1988 designed to protect drinking water quality, in response to an EC Directive on this subject. Amongst other things, this controls certain agricultural activities alongside water courses and other sources of drinking water. For example, there are constraints on spreading manure and fertilizers, storing livestock wastes, disposing of agricultural waste materials, etc.

The *UK* is introducing a system of Nitrate Sensitive Areas (NSAs) as an experimental means of controlling nitrate leaching in vulnerable catchments. There are 10 areas averaging about 1000 ha in which a voluntary management agreement approach is being taken. Farmers are offered compensation on an annual basis in return for changes in management, including limits on fertilizer application, an obligation to minimize the area of bare land in the winter and better management of organic manure. In each NSA, a basic scheme and a more restrictive "premium" scheme is offered to farmers with compensation based on expected reductions in income. In a further nine areas, the Ministry of Agriculture aims to achieve a reduction in nitrate leaching by means of an intensified programme of specialized advice to farmers.

Greece is considering the designation of water catchment areas as special zones in which either incentives or levies could be used to encourage more appropriate land use.

In 1988 the Commonwealth Government of *Australia* decided to remove its fertilizer subsidy, which had been in operation almost continuously since 1963. There remains a need to promote sustainable practices which ensure that the nutrient status of soils is maintained.

In *Canada* fertilizers are registered before sale and use. Certain polluting agricultural practices are controlled locally through land use regulations. Application of the Polluter-Pays Principle to non-point agricultural pollution is particularly difficult and development work is active in trying to find suitable instruments in this respect. Increased fertilizer use is not being promoted.

The USDA Water Quality Program is developing new management systems that reduce environmental loads of contaminants from farm chemicals and waste products while maintaining farm productivity. Economic incentives to reduce fertilizer application only rarely have been considered in the *US*; a voluntary, management plan, approach to fertilizer and pesticides use still predominates. There are, however, a few localised instances of fertilizer regulation imposed by State and local authorities, rather than Federal government. For example, Iowa has imposed a small charge on nitrogen fertilizer use, and research on reducing the harmful effects of excessive use of fertilizers is active. The USDA has a pilot cost-sharing programme to encourage farmers to reduce fertilizer (and pesticide) use. Also, Iowa has restricted the use of the herbicide atrazine. Permitted application rates were reduced from 4 lbs/acre to 3 lbs/acre in normal use and to 1.5 lbs/acre where it had been detected in groundwater. No use is allowed within 50 feet of sinkholes, wells, lakes or other water surfaces.

Similar moves are apparent in *Japan.* Traditionally, manure has been the most important fertilizer but the use of artificial fertilizers has grown. Techniques are now being developed to reduce fertilizer use by using root nodule bacteria. Registration standards have been set for all agricultural chemicals, including fertilizers, and only those that meet these standards can be sold.

New Zealand notes that no subsidies have been paid for the dominant fertilizer input (superphoshate) since 1986-87. There is little evidence available to determine a direct link between the removal of fertilizer subsidies and water quality trends. No controls on fertilizer use have been introduced.

3.4.5. *Constraints on pesticide use*

Most OECD countries have an extensive range of mechanisms for influencing and regulating the use of pesticides in agriculture and in other applications. These include registration schemes to permit the marketing and use of individual products within a country or region, controls and recommendations over the use of pesticides, safety and environmental standards applying to the manufacture, distribution and application of pesticides and policies addressing residue and waste disposal. Standards for permitted levels of residues in food (including manufactured products) and water are usual in OECD countries, often making reference to international standards. Several countries are actively encouraging the development of integrated pest management (IPM) and some have definite plans or targets for reducing pesticide usage.

While there is considerable variation in pesticide policies, most have objectives which combine concern for human health and the environment with considerations of economic efficiency and appropriate use of different products. Every country relies on a set of policies rather than a single instrument and not all the measures in place directly constrain the use of pesticides; some positively encourage the use of certain products, including alternatives to conventional agrochemicals. Nevertheless, there are clear trends towards tightening registration standards, restricting the use of certain products, especially those associated with water pollution and regulating use more precisely. This section reviews some recent developments in pesticide use across the whole spectrum of measures available, apart from taxes and levies which are addressed in Section 3.4.3.

In the EC there is a growing trend towards Community-wide legislation on pesticides. For some years there has been legislation concerning residues in foodstuffs, and concentrations in drinking water. One Directive agreed in 1990 seeks to harmonize maximum residue levels in fruit, vegetables and other plant products throughout the EC, covering pre-harvest and post-harvest treatment in a single piece of legislation. Discussions continue on a proposal which seeks to establish a single Community system of pesticide registration to replace the national systems now in force; the aim is to allow free trade in both pesticide and pesticide products throughout the Community. Pesticides already on the market would be allowed to remain in circulation but a 10-year pro-gramme of review would be initiated.

Developments in pesticide policy occurred in many European countries during the late 1980s with an overall trend towards tightening existing registration and use standards and giving greater priority to the control of residues in food and water. However, the emphasis varies considerably. Some countries, such as *Denmark* and the *Netherlands* have comprehensive programmes designed to reduce the consumption of pesticides in agriculture. Others such as *Greece* and *Portugal* are more concerned with improving the application of pesticides and storage on farms. Most countries have taken action over individual products which are causing concern. For example, the herbicide atrazine has been found in significant quantities in groundwater in several countries; in *Italy* the use and sale of this product has been banned temporarily, in *France* the Ministry of Agriculture and trade organisations have collaborated to introduce guidelines on the use of atrazine in order to protect water supplies. In *Austria* atrazine is also banned, together with certain other products and a comprehensive new law on plant protection was passed in 1990, covering the registration, licensing and handling of pesticides.

In *Denmark,* the two most notable lines of policy are the re-registration of pesticides licensed before 1980 and the implementation of the Action Plan to Reduce Pesticide Application. Re-registration is required by legislation enacted in 1987 and which is intended to prevent the continued use of pesticides which are significantly toxic, carcinogenic, highly mobile in soil, slowly decaying or liable to cause embryonic or genetic changes. Re-registration is expected to lead to the withdrawal from the market by September 1993 of a quarter of the products licensed before 1980.

The 1986 Action Plan to Reduce Pesticide Application calls for a 25 per cent reduction in total pesticide application by 1990 and a 50 per cent fall by 1997, based on average use in 1981-85. Application is defined both in terms of total active ingredients and the number of treatments. The first target has been reached, partly because of a general trend towards the use of smaller quantities of biologically active ingredients. Changes in agricultural practice have taken place and many farmers are now applying dosages below those recommended by the manufacturer, since independent field trials have shown lower doses to be cost-effective in many cases. However, the target for reductions in the number of treatments made to crops is still far from being reached. The Action Plan relies mainly on research and improved advisory services as a means of meeting the targets, but other measures may be required to meet the 1997 target.

The *Netherlands* takes the view that neither of the conventional restrictions on pesticide use (quality standards for produce and codes of good practice for farmers) is suitable for achieving substantial reductions in the levels of use. The government is therefore developing a strategic "Multi-year Plan for Crop Protection" as the framework for a planned reduction of structural dependence on pesticides. The strategy is included in the government's Memorandum on Agricultural Structures produced in 1989. The approach is similar to that adopted in *Denmark.*

The 1989 Multi-year Plan sets strategic targets for a 50 per cent reduction overall in the use of pesticides by the year 2000, with the most critical products for ground water pollution being phased out by 1994. The approval criteria for pesticides will be tightened up, the main points of concern being persistence, leaching into groundwater and toxicity to water and soil organisms.

A levy on pesticides is planned which will aim to raise 35 million guilders for use in pesticide-reduction action programmes. For example, it is intended to develop plans in cooperation with the agricultural sector, as far as possible, with the objective of reducing the use of soil disinfectants by 80-90 per cent by the year 2000.

Integrated cultivation systems (combining chemical, biological and mechanical control techniques and requiring less use of pesticides) will be developed and promoted. These systems have produced a 40 per cent decrease in insecticide use in recent years. Plans include financial incentives to farmers who introduce such methods with the objective of making integrated systems universal in the arable and plant-based sectors by 2000.

Other EC Member States, such as *Germany* and the *UK* have put greater emphasis on revised registration and use procedures, training requirements and the development of advice. Legislation in the *UK* is supplemented by statutory Codes of Practice which contain advice. The government is spending over £20 million per year on research and development particularly aimed at reducing pesticide usage. It also aims, by a voluntary approach, to ensure that pesticide usage is limited to the minimum necessary for effective control of pests compatible with human health and the environment. In the *UK* the full costs of pesticide approval and monitoring of residues in food and wildlife are funded by fees and levies on approval holders.

Germany has introduced a system of product registration which limits the clearance of some products to 10 years and has a comprehensive new law on pesticide application and use dating from 1988, which, *inter alia,* controls some products in water pollution zones and others in nature protection areas. The agriculture and environment ministries are working together to produce a catalogue of measures to reduce the inputs of pesticides into water, and products found in groundwater have been subject to greater limitations on use or outright bans in some cases. In 1990, 28 substances were prohibited entirely. The use of pesticides in some parts of *Germany* has been suspended entirely because of set-aside and extensification programmes which are more widespread than in other EC countries, but still account for only 2-3 per cent of the agricultural area.

In *Norway* a restricted number of pesticides are registered for use in agriculture. Registration is for a period of five years only. To stay on the approved list a product has to establish its superiority over other pesticides available.

In *Sweden,* there is a far-reaching programme designed to reduce the risks to human health and the environment from pesticides. The target of halving the consumption of pesticides by 1990, measured from a base of average consumption of active ingredients in 1981-85, was achieved. The measures taken include a revised system of pesticide legislation, which incorporates a risk/benefit evaluation and a five-year limit on the validity of certificates of approval, on the expiration of which the need for the pesticide must be reviewed. A new programme has been decided upon to achieve a further 50 per cent reduction by the year 1996, taking 1990 as the base year. At present, farmers are being encouraged to use lower dosages, as they are in *Denmark,* especially for weed control. A programme to pass on information to farmers on suitable dosage rates is underway.

Other measures include mandatory training for operators of spray equipment, new regulations on pesticide handling, a mandatory type test on sprayers introduced in 1991 and a system of charges on pesticides (referred to in Section 3.4.3).

At present, pesticide legislation and regulatory activities in *Canada* are being reviewed and a wide range of issues are being considered, including revised registration procedures, the role of alternatives to chemical pesticides and pesticide reduction programmes. There has been some success with integrated pest management (IPM) and education programmes are being promoted. At the provincial level IPM programmes are available for many commodities. The Ontario government, in its Food Systems 2000 programme, is promoting the reduction in use of agricultural chemicals through advisory services to farmers and others (with a target of 50 per cent reduction in total pesticides over 15 years).

More generally, *Canada* has seen voluntary reduction in pesticide use, driven by low commodity prices, in the last five years.

Australia has identified varying quality standards between the States for agricultural and veterinary chemicals as a significant problem. A number of policy initiatives in this area were under way in 1990, designed to achieve optimum efficiency in the use of chemicals, so as to minimise residues. For example, an Integrated Action Plan to control and restrict the use of organochlorines has been initiated. Rural Industry Research Funds are promoting research targeted at non-chemical pest control measures, minimum application rates and/or biological pest control.

A large number of measures has been adopted recently in the *US* to control further the use of pesticides. Legislation has constantly been before Congress, with a number of enactments. These efforts are aimed at reducing pesticide application, setting standards, monitoring effects, and requiring food label warnings. The President has personally stressed the importance of developing new national policies that recognise environmental concerns in this field, and integrated pest management programmes are implemented on 70 million acres of crops. A new system of obligatory record keeping for certified applicators of restricted use pesticides was introduced in the 1990 Food, Agriculture, Conservation and Trade Act. The amounts of State funding for IPM has grown, as has research support. The *US,* like *Canada,* subscribes to and gives very high priority to the Codex Alimentarius which attempts internationally to harmonize pesticide standards with regard to foodstuffs.

In *Japan* a number of new policies on pesticides control have been developed in recent years, notably the Agricultural Chemicals Regulation Law. Registered standards for the use of agricultural chemicals have been developed based on this law, and certain pesticides are banned. In addition, standards for preventing environmental effects have been set. Integrated Pest Management is active, both in terms of research and implementation (*e.g.* the use of pheromone, sterilised insects and weak toxic viruses).

New Zealand is considering introducing a tax on pesticides and has also investigated the establishment of differential fees for pesticides to discriminate between chemicals according to their potential to degrade the environment.

3.4.6. Constraints on the use of water in agriculture

In *Australia* irrigation is crucial to many inland agricultural areas, including in the Murray-Darling basin. Aspects of agriculture here are recognised as being unsustainable at present owing mainly to salinisation. A Natural Resource Management Strategy for the basin has been developed to promote sustainability. The Commonwealth Government is also pursuing complementary water pricing policies that should help to prevent environmental degradation. A recent government report on drought emphasises that this is a natural recurring phenomenon and that climate variability is a risk that has to be taken into account in managing rural enterprises. The Commonwealth Government also supports the development of an effective and efficient approach to water quality management.

The Australian Water Resources Council is currently developing a national strategy for sustainable water quality management. The strategy relies heavily on the adoption of nationally consistent principles for water quality management rather than the use of prescriptive measures. While providing for a shared national objective, this offers maximum flexibility for responding to diverse circumstances and needs at state, regional and local levels. This focus on desired environmental outcomes rather than a rule book approach is similar to that of the *New Zealand* Resource Management Act, which gives regional councils the authority to establish and enforce regional water management plans.

In the *US* severe restrictions on water use have been imposed as a result of drought conditions in some states.

Consideration is being given to the designation of water catchment areas as special zones in *Greece*. The use of incentives or levies to encourage more appropriate land use would also be linked to this proposal.

3.5.   *Output subsidies*

Output subsidies have significant implications for the environment (as discussed in Chapter 2). There are relatively few cases where environmental objectives have been a significant influence on changes in the overall pattern of output subsidies. In some cases new output subsidies with a clear environmental component have been introduced but few of these have been on a sufficient scale to alter the overall pattern of output subsidies, which continue to be directed more towards production than resource conservation.

In *Canada* the entire agricultural policy framework is being reviewed and a taskforce has examined income stabilisation programmes with particular attention paid to "production-neutral" income support measures. Insurance requirements for new and minor crops have been eased to encourage diversification. Compensation for crop damage caused by migratory waterfowl has been made statutory and has been enhanced.

More generally, eligibility criteria for participating in price and income support programmes in *Canada* do not include mandatory adherence to environmental conditions. Adjustments have not been made to these programmes to target price or income support to environmental need although the matter is being studied at the present time; one concern is that cross-compliance systems should not destabilise income support programmes.

In contrast, cross-compliance has become an important feature of agricultural support programmes for arable crops in the *US*. This requires that environmental objectives, principally for soil erosion control and wetland preservation, must be met in order for farmers to qualify for income support benefits. Generally, the farmer needs to change production practices in order to be in compliance.

Since 1985 there have been several programmes providing income support payments to farmers and landowners for the maintenance and improvement of environmental quality and these have been enhanced significantly by new provisions in the 1990 Food, Agriculture, Conservation and Trade Act. Under this Act, the Conservation Reserve

Programme (CRP) has been expanded and broadened to bring in a wider range of environmental objectives, including groundwater protection and surface water improvement. The programmes have been introduced against a background of generally falling levels of agricultural support, which have been encouraging crop diversification.

There are also other programmes in the *US* at the state level which have introduced a linkage between output subsidies and environmental policies; one example is the Minnesota RIM Programme which encourages the retirement of marginal land from production.

In *New Zealand* subsidies underpinning product prices have been removed; most of those remaining can be classified as "decoupled". *New Zealand* has gone further in this direction than any other OECD country, although environmental objectives played a small part in this decision. The environmental effects of this development have included a substantial fall in stocking densities and in the use of inputs such as fertilizers.

Australia generally has no price or income support arrangements for primary products; tariffs are generally low and are being further reduced. The Government's "Policies for Growth" statement of 1988 stated a major objective as being lower levels of assistance/protection to enhance competitiveness.

In Europe there have been limited steps towards reducing price supports in several countries but, on the whole, they remain at a high level, both inside the EC and in other countries. In the EC a system of "stabilisers" has been introduced in an effort to control expenditure on market support measures. This has resulted in falling production prices for some commodities, such as cereals, in most countries and some resulting pressure for crop diversification. However, the level of expenditure on the market support components of the Common Agricultural Policy (CAP) remains above the targets which have been set and substantial changes in the CAP are now being discussed, including a possible reduction in support prices accompanied by decoupled compensatory measures paid per hectare of land in production.

In *Sweden,* there has been a decision to reduce market support for agricultural products substantially, while many environmental standards are being tightened. It is expected that the process of deregulation will reduce the consumption of inputs, including agrochemicals, lead to a fall in land prices and have a generally favourable effect on the rural environment. However, new output subsidies have been introduced to encourage farmers to produce biomass, rather than food crops, on arable land. There will also be an increase in direct support for agriculture where landscape conservation, the maintenance of biodiversity or other factors are judged to require the continuation of farming.

There are a growing number of schemes whereby farmers are offered incentives for farming within agreed environmental guidelines. Some of these were discussed in Section 3.3.2. In the EC, for example, a scheme was introduced in 1988 whereby Member States are to offer farmers incentives for "extensification".

3.6. Output constraints

The most commonly used output constraint in OECD countries is marketing quotas. Several countries use this approach in the dairy sector for example. There is little evidence that quota systems have been amended in recent years to take more account of their environmental implications. Quota levels and rules are determined more by other considerations, such as market availability, farm incomes, etc.

Some recent policies are designed to restrain output by influencing the system of farm management or the use of inputs. Most prominent of these are set-aside policies (described in Section 3.4.1). Other policies in this category include those designed to encourage low input and organic farming.

3.7. *Environmental regulation*

A large number of new environmental regulations have been introduced in OECD countries in the last three years and some of these have an impact on the agriculture sector. Many effectively impose constraints of some kind on the practices which farmers can adopt. A few are intended to provide agriculture with protection from environmental damage originating in other sectors, for example the disposal of toxic waste on agricultural land.

A significant proportion of the more important environmental regulations concerning agriculture relate to the use of individual inputs, particularly pesticides, fertilizers, manure and machinery. A number of these have been referred to in Section 3.4. However, many regulations form part of an overall policy designed to address a particular problem such as the safe and efficient use of pesticides. Such policies may have several different components. Pesticide policy, for example, may include regulations affecting product registration, controls on suppliers and users of pesticides and those disposing of wastes, advisory and research activities, incentives for adopting alternative practices, food quality monitoring and control, etc. In this sense, environmental regulations often extend beyond the imposition of input constraints to form a broader set of influences on the agricultural sector.

One group of environmental regulations which are not focused on inputs into agriculture are those concerned with undesirable outputs such as noise, waste products, odours, etc. Many OECD countries have regulations controlling waste products from intensive livestock farms particularly. In the *Netherlands,* for example, a target has been set for a 70 per cent reduction in ammonia emissions from 1980 levels by the year 2000. In *Sweden* a 25 per cent reduction in ammonia emissions from livestock farms by the year 1995 has been decided upon and this may be extended to a 50 per cent reduction target for the year 2000. Smoke from the burning of waste products such as straw and stubble can give rise to air pollution. *Denmark* prohibited stubble burning from 1990 and new regulations are coming into force in the *UK* which will lead to a ban from 1993.

3.7.1. *Nature conservation*

An area of environmental policy which usually contains a range of components likely to impinge on different aspects of agriculture is that of nature conservation, including the protection of fauna, flora and their habitats.

Measures in this category often have an important impact on agriculture because farming occupies a large proportion of the land area in many OECD countries. The appropriate management of farm land may be an important means of achieving nature conservation and landscape protection goals. Usually, these policies are pursued most intensively within designated or protected areas which have been defined because of their particular environmental importance but their application in the wider countryside is growing in many countries. Many of the policies entail constraints or prohibitions on specified farming activities or developments, which may or may not be accompanied by compensation or other aid. In several countries, there are incentives for positive landscape and habitat management.

In *Norway* a special landscape preservation programme is expected to be introduced in 1991. This is an extension of the ordinary acreage and cultural landscape support scheme, but will be directed more towards areas with special cultural landscape qualities. The support is organised as a management agreement between the farmers and the government. The aim is to encourage farmers to maintain, develop and improve ecological, historical and aesthetic landscape qualities. In 1991 20 million Nkr is expected to be available for this programme, which may be increased in the future.

In *Denmark* about four per cent of the agricultural area has been designated as "Environmentally Sensitive Areas" on a quarter of which management agreements will be arranged, mainly to encourage extensive grazing. In addition, a Nature Management Act was passed in 1989 with wildlife conservation, landscape improvement, afforestation and improved recreation as the main objectives. In addition to management agreements, land acquisition, public afforestation projects and subsidies to environmentally favourable practices will be used to advance the aims. One component is expected to be the reestablishment of important habitats and landscape features such as lakes and meadows, and naturally meandering streams and rivers (reversing canalisation works). The limits of this programme will be determined largely by the budget, at present around 900 million Dkr over a five-year period.

In *Portugal* there is a prohibition against removing cork oaks, and some vines, olive trees and green oaks are protected as well. There are also income compensation payments available over a period of sixty years for the planting of cork trees.

In *Sweden* there are various measures which oblige or encourage farmers to maintain or avoid destroying habitats. Grants of 300-600 Skr per hectare per annum are available for farmers maintaining particularly valuable grazing and wooded meadows. In 1989 30 000 ha were protected by a total grant of 20 million Skr, which was extended to 40 million Skr from 1990. In the same year a new programme was introduced to promote landscape variation in the lowlands.

The highly erodible land and wetland conservation provisions of the *US* 1985 Food Security Act, popularly known as the "sod buster" and "swamp buster" provisions, deny USDA farm programme benefits to those who convert highly erodible range, pasture, and forestland or wetlands for crop production. These provisions help check the influx of highly erodible cropland that might otherwise take place because of land retirement through the Conservation Reserve Program and contribute to the proposed "no net loss" of wetlands goal announced in 1989. However, progress on implementing the 1974 Endangered Species Act has been variable, being slow with regard to pesticides for example. In 1988/89, the EPA attempted to implement the Act with regard to restricting pesticide use in designated aras, but the development of practical means of implementing this Act is still underway.

Although wildlife protection formerly did not receive major attention in *Japan,* there has been a growing interest in this issue. Prefectural governors as well as central government have the power to designate wildlife protection zones. Central government can provide resources to local authorities to purchase land for reserves, but so far this has occurred infrequently.

To conserve and protect wildlife, *Canada* is following up on several research policy initiatives regarding wildlife science, health research, wetlands, wildlife population and biodiversity which may interact with agricultural policies and practices. In addition to the North American Waterfowl Management Plan, which focuses on wetland conservation, there are some Canadian provincial programmes aimed at the safeguarding of endangered plant or animal species. Since 1989 the RENEW Committee (Recovery of Nationally Endangered Wildlife) has prioritised 25 species, formed seven recovery teams and prepared three recovery plans. By autumn 1991, 25 recovery plans are expected to have been approved.

Some provinces in *Canada* have implemented wetland protection policies designed to prevent further wetland loss. Currently the federal government is developing a federal policy on wetland conservation.

In *Australia*, the Commonwealth Government has decided to fund an Environmental Resource Information Network to catalogue endangered species, vegetation types and heritage sites. Wetland conservation and management issues are being considered at a national level by water and nature conservation ministerial councils (of Commonwealth and State Ministries). Responsibility for wetland management is at the State level and several States are developing wetland management policies.

In *New Zealand*, the Department of Conservation has primary responsibility for the protection and conservation of the country's historic and natural resources, including wildlife habitat and landscape protection. There is a longstanding programme of controls for introduced animals and pest management.

3.7.2. Soil protection measures

Soil protection is another area of policy in which a wide variety of different instruments and approaches are utilised. The objectives of policy vary considerably between OECD countries with an emphasis on soil erosion in *North America, Australia, New Zealand, Spain and Portugal* while the protection of soils from contamination, pollution and degradation is a more pressing priority in several European countries.

In *Australia* there has been a growing awareness of the interdependence of social, economic and technical policies concerned with natural resource management (including soils, water, vegetation, biodiversity, etc.) leading to the establishment of a policy framework based on a whole systems approach to sustainable land use. This involves agencies at all levels of government together with landusers and the community generally. In 1989 the ''LandCare'' initiative was launched. This builds on the ''National Soil Conservation Strategy'' which aims to ensure that the nation's lands are used within their capability and managed in an integrated way using practices which conserve Australia's soil resources.

There are three components of the policy. The first is ''the year and decade of Landcare'' which aims to improve awareness, participation and education efforts, with the objectives of establishing a national land degradation control programme. To this end, a process is in train to develop a national Decade of Landcare Plan. Other elements of Landcare include a review of other policies, and increased funding for the National Soil Conservation Programme. This initiative complements a number of existing programmes, such as the ''One Billion Trees'' and ''Save the Bush'' programmes and the Murray-Darling River Basin initiative, which are intended to utilise community interests and efforts. Tax incentives for soil conservation also have been reviewed and are being amended to encourage prevention of land degradation.

The National Soil Conservation Programme was announced in *Canada* in December 1987 and has been implemented across the country in subsequent years. Information on soil quality is being improved and an environmental assessment review process will be implemented at research establishments throughout the country. In addition, soil and water protection measures are important features of many of the Canadian regional development initiatives, with an emphasis on reducing degradation and making better use of farm resources.

The *US* has had a 50 year history of Federal and State support for soil conservation. Conservation policies have supported voluntary adoption by farmers of soil erosion control measures with some cost-sharing and other financial assistance. These efforts have had some effect on water quality. However, the emphasis on on-farm productivity in the past has limited the effectiveness of these erosion control measures in protecting water quality.

A number of recent policy changes have led to soil erosion policies which incorporate off-farm water quality protection. The USDA recently has redirected its soil conservation programmes to place greater emphasis on provisions to support soil erosion control with water quality protection as programme objectives. However, much of the responsibility and initiative for non-point source water pollution control lies with the States. The 1987 Water Quality Act required the States to develop non-point source pollution control programmes to protect surface water quality; many of them have developed soil erosion control programmes which reduce or prevent water pollution from cropland runoff.

In *Austria, Germany, the Netherlands* and *Switzerland,* the concept of soil protection has been developed as an approach to integrating policies with an impact on soil quality. In *Austria,* for example, the concept was developed in a document published in 1989 which sets out aims and strategic measures. The first step in implementation is a national inventory of important soil characteristics being compiled by the Bundesländer (regions) following federal guidelines. This will include data on contaminants such as heavy metals.

In many European countries, one recent concern has been the control of sewage sludge disposal on agricultural land. EC Member States were required to comply with a Directive introducing controls over this method of disposal of sewage sludge by July 1989. The main purpose is to control the accumulation of heavy metals, such as cadmium and nickel in agricultural soils. New legislation or codes of practice have been drawn up in several countries. Outside the EC, *Sweden* is also addressing this issue.

3.8. The polluter-pays principle

3.8.1. Application of the polluter-pays principle to agriculture

The Polluter-Pays Principle (PPP) was defined in an OECD Recommendation adopted on 26 May 1972 on ''Guiding principles concerning international economic aspects of environmental policies'' (C(72)12). The definition takes as a premise that ''public measures are ... necessary to reduce pollution and to reach a better allocation of resources by ensuring that prices of goods depending on the quality and/or quantity of environmental resources reflect more closely their relative scarcity and that economic agents concerned react accordingly''. The PPP means that ''the polluter should bear the expenses of carrying out the above mentioned measures decided by public authorities to ensure that the environment is in an acceptable state. In other words, the cost of these measures should be reflected in the cost of goods and services which cause pollution in production and/or consumption''.

Several countries are paying closer attention to the application of the PPP to the agriculture sector. Many have found that there are considerable difficulties in applying the Principle effectively to agriculture, especially in the case of non-point source pollution. The indisputable identification of polluters and polluting practices is difficult in many situations. The costs and feasibility of effective monitoring and control, and the high cost involved in significantly changing certain farm practices, have tended to militate against strict enforcement of the PPP in agriculture. In addition, the particular features of the agricultural sector, such as the large number of relatively small individual producers and the important role of public subsidies, have discouraged many governments from seeking to apply the PPP very vigorously. The trend is towards the greater use of regulations, usually involving some costs to farmers, but sometimes accompanied by compensation. Most of the other initiatives which have been made have involved the introduction of economic instruments, such as taxes on inputs, and the raising of revenues to contribute to the costs of government programmes.

In *Turkey*, both agricultural and environmental policy objectives have been defined recently in the preparatory document for the fifth Five Year Development Plan. Although there is no integration between agricultural and environmental policy objectives, one innovation has been the inclusion in the agricultural objectives of a new policy to give attention to the need to avoid routing roads, water, electricity, oil and gas pipelines through agricultural land. The Environment Law formally adopts the Polluter-Pays Principle and provides that polluters will be held responsible, not only for the costs of preventing pollution but also for any contamination or damage which they have caused or further damage arising from pollution incidents. This principle applies irrespective of whether the polluter was at fault in causing the incident.

The EC Commission has stated that the PPP should apply to agriculture, but in conjunction with other measures. Some Member States state that they adhere to PPP for agriculture in principle (*e.g. Greece, UK*) but it is not strictly applied in practice in any EC country.

The *Canadian* approach to implementing the PPP has been cautious so far but is evolving, as is the use of cross-compliance systems. There has been an emphasis on regulation and legislation supported by appropriate education and extension systems rather than the use of economic instruments for promoting integration.

The *Australian* approach to the PPP is that each producer and consumer should be responsible for the costs which their activities impose on themselves, others and future generations. But full application of the PPP in agriculture and elsewhere has been hampered by lack of knowledge of the long term effects of some activities, and the problems of identifying pollution sources.

In *Japan* entrepreneurs can be required to pay for restoration work carried out by municipalities and also must bear the costs of compliance with environmental regulations. Otherwise the PPP is not applied, but neither is there compensation for the owners of facilities causing pollution, including livestock units, if they are closed down or their use is restricted.

The PPP is not widely applied in agriculture in the *US*. Reliance is placed more on voluntary programmes involving some form of positive financial incentive. However, cross-compliance gradually is becoming more common, especially in relation to price and income support systems and set-aside policies.

In *Norway* the PPP is accepted but its application in agriculture is currently being examined. The most important question under discussion is whether environmental costs should be carried by the agricultural sector as a whole or as costs put on the individual farmer. A possible means of implementing the principle would be for farmers to pay for a considerable part of the necessary environmental investments and adjustments, while the agricultural sector as a whole is compensated for its loss of income.

The use of investment subsidies and loans in order to improve the environmental effects of agricultural production is also under discussion. It is being debated whether such payments are to be regarded as subsidies to the polluter, and therefore represent a violation of the PPP.

3.9. Institutional and procedural mechanisms

3.9.1. Institutional mechanisms

The alteration of administrative responsibilities and the development of new agencies and linkages often are important elements in improving policy integration. In many OECD countries there have been changes in and redefinition of the responsibilities or missions of the agriculture or environment ministries; in some cases wholly new agencies have been established. Inter-ministerial working groups, task forces, joint initiatives and shared responsibility for implementation, regular review meetings and amended monitoring procedures are some of the administrative adjustments that have been made.

More extensive consultation inside and outside government has taken place prior to final policy agreement in several countries. Farming organisations, environmental agencies, NGOs, interest groups, indigenous people and scientific bodies have been amongst those playing a larger role in policy development and management planning. New procedures have included the wider use of environmental impact assessment and similar tools for project or policy review and more integrated forms of land and water use planning. Public hearings and inquiries, parliamentary review, policy research and assessment and similar measures are being used to introduce a stronger environmental element into agricultural policy.

The wide ranging review of agricultural and environmental policies that has taken place in *Canada* has spawned a series of assessments of past policy and new plans for the future. Several new procedures have been implemented and the goal is to work towards natural resource accounting.

Recent institutional changes at the federal government level range from the establishment of new environmental Cabinet Committees, strengthening environmental assessment procedures, a national Round Table on Sustainable Development and a set of criteria for the assessment of environmental sustainability, to the establishment of new inter-departmental committees and taskforces. The Federal Department of Agriculture has just established the ''Bureau of Environmental Sustainability'' to spearhead and co-ordinate the work of integrating environmental considerations throughout the agri-food sector.

In the *US* numerous memoranda of understanding have been agreed to between federal agencies. These memoranda cover information exchange, co-operation on policy setting and monitoring and the establishment of joint databases.

Under the 1990 FACTA, a new Agricultural Council on Environmental Quality (ACEQ) and an Office of Environmental Quality will be established in the Department of Agriculture. The ACEQ will be responsible for co-ordinating and directing all environmental policies and programmes of the Department.

In *Australia* the Commonwealth Government has developed guidelines for Ministers' decisions on resource use, including those on an integrated approach, optimising net returns to society from the nation's resources and promoting multiple resource use. The guidelines are intended to provide the framework for integrating conservation and development issues.

One of the most widespread developments has been an expansion in the role or capacity of agricultural authorities. For example, in the EC the portfolio of the Commissioner for Agriculture was expanded to incorporate rural development issues in 1989. Departmental changes have also occurred. In *Greece* the agricultural ministry's Directorate of Plant Protection has been reorganised and a section on Biological and Integrated Pest Management established. In the case of *New Zealand*, the corporate contract of the Ministry of Agriculture and Fisheries identifies a number of outcomes sought, including sustainable production systems and optimum land use, economic self-reliance of agricultural producers and industries, healthy rural communities and the efficient management of resources entrusted to the agency. The functional structure of the agency has been reorganised to achieve these objectives.

The implementation of new measures which combine agricultural and environmental aims, such as Article 19 of EC Regulation 797/85, inevitably result in practical collaboration between agencies. In *France,* proposals for eligible areas are passed from the Département level to the national level where administrative procedures have been introduced to draw on the advice of the Ministry of the Environment and of nature protection associations. For this purpose, a new Agriculture and Environment Technical Committee has been created. In the *UK,* the Ministry of Agriculture has a legal obligation to work with the Countryside Commission and Nature Conservancy Council in establishing its policy on Environmentally Sensitive Areas.

There are many examples of Joint Committees formed by agricultural and environment ministries, such as that established to run the nitrate programme in *France* or make proposals on agriculture and water protection in *Finland.*

3.9.2. *Environmental impact assessment (EIA)*

In *Canada*, new systems have been established for environmental assessment. It is now a requirement that all federal agricultural policy and programme proposals receive an environmental impact assessment early in the planning stage. This complements the requirement instituted in 1984 that all physical projects should be assessed under the Environmental Assessment Review Process (EARP). Moreover, all existing and future federal and provincial agricultural programmes will be reviewed to ensure that they do not contribute inadvertently to environmental degradation. In the *US* water contract renewals for irrigation water are conditional on the preparation of an Environmental Impact Statement certifying that the renewal should not significantly damage the natural environment.

Many EC Member States have been introducing new or amended legislation or administrative procedures concerning EIA. This is partly because of an obligation to comply with an EC Directive (85/337) by July 1988, a deadline which was missed in many cases. The EC Directive covers a number of agricultural developments, such as land consolidation schemes and drainage works, if they could have a "significant" effect on the environment.

National and sometimes regional legislation implements the EC directive in various ways. In the Flanders region of *Belgium,* for example, there are detailed definitions of the scale and nature of developments requiring an EIA, whereas in the Wallonia region the system is far less specific. In *Portugal,* where afforestation of declining habitats is a major environmental concern, schemes involving fast-growing species of over 350 ha in area require an EIA. The corresponding figure for *Ireland* is 200 ha.

The EC Commission is currently considering proposing an amendment to the Directive to tighten its application to agricultural and forestry projects.

In *Sweden*, the Environment Protection Agency and the Planning and Housing Board have recently examined the possibility of a more systematic use of environmental impact assessment with agriculture one of the sectors being considered. In January 1989, a new ordinance on EIA came into force in *Switzerland* applying, *inter alia,* to comprehensive land improvement schemes affecting 400 hectares or more and large new intensive livestock units.

3.10. *Monitoring and evaluation*

Some degree of environmental monitoring takes place in all OECD countries, with responsibilities often divided between different institutions and between different levels of government. In many countries, such as *Germany* and *Switzerland,* much of the monitoring takes place at a local or regional level. A number of countries are taking steps towards the better integration and accessibility of data sources on the environment, which will make them more useful for policy development purposes. *Australia* and the *US* have both undertaken significant reorganisation leading to improved integration during the last three years. The possibility also exists in *New Zealand* as indicated by the reforms introduced in the Resource Management Act.

Assembling the information required to reduce pollution from agricultural sources and to develop environmentally sensitive agriculture adapted to local conditions can be a substantial task entailing major expense. This is true in the *US* where cost factors make it particularly desirable to make best use of the information available. The kind of steps required are the establishment of co-ordinated national databases and the development of uniform and improved methods of sampling measurement and evaluations. Some countries recently have completed databases, for example the inventory of interesting zones for flora and fauna in *France* was finished in 1990.

The principal subjects of monitoring include water, soil and air quality, status of threatened or rare fauna and flora, plant health, the use of agrochemicals and fertilisers, the extent of erosion, protection of native species and habitats, etc. Many countries have made increased commitments to water quality monitoring, often giving greater attention to pollution from agricultural sources, particularly of nitrates, phosphates and pesticides. In *Denmark*, for example, a national monitoring programme, measuring nitrogen, phosphorous and organic matter in the aquatic environment was started in 1988. This is based on 255 monitoring stations on streams and rivers, 68 groundwater monitoring points and measurement of concentrations at 37 selected lakes. Some coastal waters are monitored also, as are a number of sources of pollutants. The programme costs 100 million Danish Kroner per annum to run. The costs of such monitoring can lead to the concentration of effort on relatively small areas, as in *Finland,* or may inhibit monitoring programmes, as in the case of groundwater in *Portugal.*

Monitoring efforts change in response to new policy priorities. Monitoring of heavy metal levels in soil has intensified in a number of countries and often this has been associated with stronger controls over the disposal of sewage sludge on agricultural land.

Few countries have reported on their monitoring and evaluation of policies; exceptions include the *UK* where most new policies, including recent environmental initiatives, are being monitored. It appears that many policy initiatives have not been thoroughly monitored or evaluated in the past, although now there is a tendency to devote more resources to this activity. In some cases, quantitative targets for reducing pollution loads or emissions have led directly to a stronger emphasis on monitoring the results of new policies. Such targets may be set nationally or at an international level. For example, a number of countries have undertaken to reduce the flow of nutrients and pesticides into the North Sea and this has led not only to research to identify the current level of such flows but also to improved monitoring and assessment of the policies adopted to meet international obligations.

3.11. *Research, education and extension*

Research, education and extension activities and programmes play an important part in supporting many of the policy objectives mentioned in earlier sections of this report. Policies to reduce the consumption of pesticides in agriculture nearly always include an important research component for example, and very often rely on education and extension programmes for farmers as well.

This research is often directly linked to education and extension programmes. In *Canada,* for example, integrated pest management (IPM) is the focus of considerable research and educational effort and provincial level IPM programmes are available for many commodities. This in turn influences advice available to farmers from different government agencies. In Ontario, the Food Systems 2000 Programme is promoting a reduction in use of agricultural chemicals to farmers through advisory services, with a target of a 50 per cent reduction in total pesticide use over 15 years. Targets for reduced pesticide use have also been set in *Denmark, the Netherlands, Sweden* and other countries, most of which rely heavily on research and advisory programmes to meet the targets.

Aside from pesticides, IPM, biological pest control, etc., other subjects of research include the better use of crop nutrients in agriculture, water quality, the development of alternative systems and low input forms of agriculture, alternative crops, biotechnology, erosion control, waste management, the control of ammonia and smells from livestock farms, soil acidification, air pollution from other sectors adversely affecting agriculture, etc.

In a few countries new agencies or institutes have been established to give a stronger emphasis to the environment. In *Norway,* for example, there is a new research institute specialising in environment and resource management problems (Jordforsk).

Many existing institutions have adopted new multi-annual research projects on agriculture and environment themes, such as INRA in *France*. In others the overall goals for agricultural research and development have been revised, as in *Japan* in January 1990.

Several countries have reported an increased budgetary commitment to environmental aspects of agricultural research. In *Germany,* for example, the Federal Ministry for Food, Agriculture and Forestry now has about 400 projects concerned with the development of environmentally friendly farming with an overall budget of around DM 95 million, about a third of the total research budget of the Ministry. A similar proportion of the research budget is devoted to this subject in other ministries with a mandate relevant to agriculture and the environment. In the *US,* the Federal budget for research on water quality rose from just over $60 million in 1990 to about $77 million in 1991, with many aspects relevant to agricultural pollution. A wide range of environmental R&D has been initiated in the *UK,* accounting for about £50 million of the total Ministry of Agriculture R&D budget of £120 million in 1991/92.

Many countries report the establishment of new courses or programmes in universities, agricultural colleges and other educational institutions with a strong environmental component. As well as being aimed at younger students, some of these courses are intended to provide training and mid career education for those already involved in the agricultural sector, especially those involved in extension work.

The form of extension services and the means whereby they are financed varies considerably between OECD countries but many have reported a stronger emphasis on the environment, particularly the control of pollution and the introduction of new and more environmentally sensitive practices.

In an effort to inform farmers of water pollution hazards, the National Advisory Service in *Ireland* has trained many of its advisers to deal with farm pollution and has organised seminars throughout the country in conjunction with farming organisations.

In the *UK* there is increasing co-ordination at a local level between government and non-government bodies concerned with advising farmers on environmental issues, especially nature conservation. Local government at County level may play a co-ordinating role and sometimes provides financial support for local projects.

In *Portugal*, the environmental ministry SEARN holds seminars at a regional level in conjunction with farmers representatives and the agricultural ministry in order to address specific environmental/farming issues. In *Greece* eight regional centres for plant protection and quality checking have been established, responsible, *inter alia*, for the control of pesticide residues. In several countries, agricultural extension services and local research stations have become more active in promoting organic and low input agriculture. For example, in *Sweden* nine government specialists on this subject are working with the extension services; organic farming also has been incorporated in the work of the County Agricultural Board extension offices.

Integration at the local level is being strengthened in the *US* by greater inter-agency co-operation, particularly associated with IPM and Conservation Reserve Programmes. In general, the extension services are focused more on environmental, rather than production raising, targets, with the development of sustainable agriculture as the overall goal. In *Japan,* where there are 11,000 extension workers, traditionally environmental concerns have been of low priority but this is now beginning to change.

3.12. External factors

A variety of developments at the international level are influencing the evolution of policy on agriculture and environment in OECD countries. One of the most important set of pressures are those exerted by international trading relations and the current discussions on bringing agriculture within GATT. Some of those countries which are lowering overall levels of support for agriculture or are reducing production incentives are doing so partly or wholly because of the changing international trading climate. Similarly, the GATT negotiations have led to an increased interest in ''decoupled'' forms of support for agriculture, including payments for farmers which are linked to the provision of environmental services. The number of such policies and the volume of expenditure which they attract is growing rapidly although it remains a small proportion of the overall cost of support in most countries.

The agricultural policies of some of the world's largest trading countries or blocs also have a significant influence on the policies of their trading partners. The discussions over reform of the EC's Common Agricultural Policy (CAP) for example have had ramifications not only for countries within the EC but also for some of those outside it.

International agreements on environmental issues are another influence on national policy development. Some of these agreements are at a broad international level such as the setting of standards by the United Nations or organisations or agencies associated with them, such as Codex Alimentarius. Some agreements are at a regional level, for example the International Conference on the Protection of the North Sea, which has led to the setting of targets for a reduced level of nutrient and toxic chemical run-off into the North Sea, in turn affecting agricultural policies in several countries with watersheds draining into the Sea. European countries with territory in the Alps have been involved in international discussions on protecting the Alpine ecosystem. This is expected to lead to agreement on a Convention on the Protection of the Alps towards the end of 1991. This Convention will include binding Protocols covering a number of subjects, one of which is mountain farming. It is one of the first such agreements to introduce specific environmental requirements for the agricultural sector.

Many OECD countries are concerned about the potential impacts of global warming over the coming decades. Several have mounted research studies to investigate the potential impact of global warming and associated meteorological changes on agricultural production. Some have also compiled inventories of greenhouse gas emissions, including those associated with agricultural production. It is clear that the potential impact of global warming will be an influence on both agricultural and environmental policies in the coming decade.

3.13. Outlook

Several OECD countries have announced policies or proposals which will lead to considerable further changes in the current array of measures concerned with agriculture and the environment. The nature of these commitments varies. Some are based on setting new objectives, such as the establishment of sustainable forms of agriculture; others are more focused on quantitative targets, such as quantifiable reductions in the volume of pesticides consumed annually. Some of the most active areas of policy are concerned with protection of water quality, preventing erosion and restoring eroded soils, and the protection of wildlife habitats, particularly wetlands. The use of biotechnology in agriculture is the focus of an emerging set of policies in several countries, as well as the subject of an expanding research programme. Interest in "alternative" agriculture is also growing and is the subject of both research and new legislative proposals. In defining and developing such new systems, environmental objectives are also involved, such as improved welfare for farm animals.

The pace at which policy advances is likely to be variable, reflecting a wide range of factors including the nature of the legislative process in individual countries. While some countries amend and develop policy on an incremental basis, others make use of multi-annual plans and programmes to redefine policy and goals. In both cases there is often a time lag between policy implementation and seeing the fruits of the new policy measure.

Although there has been some movement towards policy integration during the period 1988-1990, it is still rather early to evaluate its impact. Monitoring and assessment of new policy initiatives has not always received a high priority and OECD countries have reported relatively few detailed assessment studies. Many of the policy initiatives referred to have more than one objective and the extent to which specifically environmental goals have been achieved is not always clear. A review of this kind which provides a brief account of a growing catalogue of measures is unavoidably selective and may omit significant developments which run counter to the general trend towards integration. Thus, it would be unwise to place too much emphasis on the pace of change observed or to exaggerate the extent of real integration that has been attained. Further evaluation is required.

Some progress over the last three years can be identified. The environmental aspects of agriculture have received greater attention almost everywhere. The changing climate for international trade in agricultural commodities and the problems of controlling surplus production in many OECD countries have contributed to, although they do not solely account for, this development. Agricultural production capacity is still being expanded in some OECD countries. Changing technologies are also contributing to a growing capacity to raise output from an agricultural land area which is shrinking in most OECD countries. However, increasing output is no longer such a central priority and the door continues to open to a wider array of objectives, of which improved environmental quality is clearly one.

Annex

Australia

The Australian Agricultural Council, which brings together the Federal and State government ministers responsible for agriculture, recently has considered a report on sustainable agriculture prepared by a special working group. Its recommendations are now being considered by the Federal and State governments and it is being used as a significant input into the national strategy on ecologically sustainable development announced by the Australian government in June 1990.

Canada

In December 1990, Canada adopted a comprehensive environmental action plan. The "Green Plan" will receive $3 billion in federal government funding over the next six years. A significant portion will be allocated to enhance environmental sustainability in the agri-food sector. Funding for the sector will be focused on the implementation of recommendations contained in the June 1990 report of the Federal-Provincial Agriculture Committee on Environmental Sustainability. It will support environmental protection and conservation measures regarding, *inter alia,* agricultural soil resources, water quality, wildlife habitat, pollution and waste management, and genetic resources.

In the same month, the government of Canada also released Recommendations for a Revised Federal Pest Management Regulatory System. The report was the result of a multi-stakeholder process, with environmentalists, farmers, chemical companies, health specialists, labour representatives, etc. all represented on the review team. The government is now examining the legal, trade, economic, environmental and resource implications of the Recommendations.

The Farm Income Protection Act (FIPA), adopted on 22 March 1991, provides a mandate for, *inter alia,* a full assessment of its possible environmental impacts and the release of a public report within two years of promulgation and again after five years. It also empowers the Minister of Agriculture to alter the terms and conditions of related farm programmes in order to mitigate any environmental impacts of the Act.

Shortly afterwards, Canada adopted new farm support and adjustment measures under the FIPA legislation. The measures include support of up to $72 million over three years to producers of grains and oilseed, and horticultural crops, for activities related to environmental protection and resource conservation.

France

A new National Plan for the Environment was adopted in December 1990. Amongst other things, this refers to the April 1990 programme on "Tomorrow's Soil" which emphasizes the necessity of integrating agriculture, protection of the environment and quality of life. Another aspect of this Plan is institutional change, with new regional environmental authorities being created shortly, taking on the personnel from the Regional Water Management Services.

CORPEN, the Orientation Committee for Reducing Water Pollution by Nitrates and Phosphates from Agricultural Sources, has established specifications for advisory services at the farm level, with the aim of modifying current fertilization practices to reduce nitrate pollution of water. The Ministry of Agriculture has initiated a new national instrument for encouraging the development of operations at the farm level, particularly by granting a new label "ferti-mieux" upon satisfactory fulfilment of CORPEN specifications. This will be administered by the National Association for Agricultural Development (ANDA), which is involved in collecting parafiscal charges on agricultural commodities used to fund advisory and applied research services. The scheme officially began in May 1991, with the Ministry of the Environment represented on the Steering Committee. At the same time, fertiliser manufacturers and distributors have signed an agreement with the Ministry of Agriculture to promote a large scale information and awareness campaign for farmers aimed at reducing excessive use of nitrogen.

It has been decided that the water pollution levy currently paid to water authorities by domestic and industrial users should be applied to certain livestock farms as well. A new levy related to nitrate pollution from all sources including agriculture may be introduced in future. Decisions on implementation will be taken progressively from 1992, during the next planning period for the water authorities.

The number of départements within France which are interested in introducing schemes under Article 19 of EC Directive 797/85 has grown considerably. Twenty three schemes have been agreed in twelve regions, all but ten in mainland France. The most attractive schemes cover the protection of biotopes, others are concerned with controlling abandonment of agricultural land and the protection of Mediterranean forests. However, schemes concerned with pollution control raise specific problems. The schemes could be developed further if current negotiations within the EC lead to the introduction of incentives for farmers who adopt or maintain environmentally sensitive practices. France has been involved actively in these negotiations.

Further steps have been taken to try to control forest fires in the Mediterranean zone, including the creation of "fire-foresters" units, measures to remove undergrowth and introduce cultivation lines to act as firebreaks in sensitive zones.

Norway

In Norway, there has been increased emphasis on measures to reduce soil erosion. In late 1990 it was decided that the 1991 budget should provide for implementation of a temporary measure designed to reduce autumn soil cultivation in erosion-vulnerable areas. In the proposal to the Storting regarding the Agricultural Agreement for 1991-92 this measure is made permanent. The measure will be supported by specific financial penalties if restrictions are not fulfilled.

Sweden

Developments in Sweden since October 1990 have included:
- the provision of funds for the development of methods for type approval and serial testing of fertilizer equipment and techniques for spreading manure and chemical fertilizers as a means of limiting nitrate leaching;
- stricter requirements for autumn and winter crop cover (50-60 per cent of the land area in the south of Sweden) as a means of limiting nitrogen leaching. Funds have been earmarked for information and pilot projects on autumn and winter crop production;
- introduction of an environmental tax on liquid ammonia;
- it has been agreed that ammonia evaporation must be reduced by 25 per cent by 1995. The potential for reducing emissions by 50 per cent before the year 2000 is being investigated;
- the Chemical Inspectorate has been authorized to investigate the possibility of establishing differentiated taxes on agricultural chemicals, set in relation to the hazardous properties of the pesticides and the risks associated with their use. Taxes on chemicals will be levied in a dose-related fashion in place of the present system which takes the form of levies per kilo of active substance purchased;
- it has been decided that the cadmium content of artificial fertilizers must be sharply reduced. A government Commissioner has been appointed to propose a tax on cadmium and a maximum permissible cadmium content in artificial fertilizers;
- it is now prohibited to dig ditches in those areas of forest and agricultural land where it is important from a nature conservation point of view to preserve wetlands;
- there is stricter enforcement of the Act on the Management of Agricultural Land, so as to more efficiently protect flora and fauna and historical pastures;
- government authorities responsible for different sectors of the economy have been given firm environmental responsibilities. The Swedish Environmental Protection Agency will serve as coordinator and central authority, and draw up general guidelines. The sectoral authorities will reformulate general environmental goals so as to specify sectoral goals and then implement the goals. The National Board of Agriculture will report annually on environmental conditions in the sector for which they are responsible;
- the environmental impact of the new agricultural policy will be monitored and assessed on a yearly basis, as will the effects, demands for and scope of subsidies being paid for creating an open and varied landscape;
- agreement on the government's long term environmental strategy was reached in 1991. Two of the main subjects are sustainable agriculture and forestry; and
- if a habitat for an endangered species (of flora or fauna) is threatened by the undertaking of a certain measure, legal proceedings now can be taken to prohibit that measure.

United Kingdom

The Countryside Stewardship Scheme, a new initiative foreshadowed in 1990, was announced in early 1991. Under a pilot scheme to run in England, incentive payments will be made to farmers and other landowners for:

- management practices designed to enhance or restore certain valued landscapes and habitats, many of which have diminished in quantity and quality in recent times; and
- improving opportunities for the public to appreciate and enjoy them.

Initially the scheme is targeted at chalk and limestone grasslands, heathland, waterside landscapes, coastal land and some upland areas.

Adoption by farmers of several environmental schemes is increasing. For example, the area of set-aside land subject to supplementary environmental management payments under the "Countryside Premium Scheme" had risen to 4,500 hectares after two years in the seven eastern counties where the scheme is in operation.

The Environmentally Sensitive Areas (ESA) scheme has been reviewed on the basis of the environmental and economic monitoring data that has been collected in order to assess the scheme's impact. This review concluded that the scheme has been successful in meeting its objectives and should continue with the aim of achieving further environmental benefits. Proposals to strengthen first round ESAs, designated in 1987, include:

- introducing payments to encourage the positive enhancement of landscape features;
- adjusting the boundaries of some ESAs;
- increasing the length of agreement from 5 to 10 years.

A similar review of ESAs designated in 1988/89 will be conducted during 1992.

United States

In November 1990, the US Congress enacted amendments to the Coastal Zone Management Act (CZMA) which address the pollution of coastal waters by non-point sources, and other coastal resource protection problems. Significantly, these amendments require the creation of state regulatory programmes for non-point source pollution control if states wish to maintain the full share of Federal funding for their coastal programmes. This is a precedent in the US. The amendments include the full range of non-point sources, both urban and rural. EPA and the USDA co-operated in the development of guidance for state programmes. The states are to have their programmes in place within three years.

The CZMA amendments also present a departure from earlier Federal water quality legislation in that they base policy recommendations and standards on the technology of controlling pollution rather than using water quality standards as a regulatory tool. The EPA has developed a set of recommended management measures which are based on application of best available nonpoint source pollution control practices or technologies. This approach is under consideration for new Clean Water Act legislation.

Finland

The general fertiliser tax in Finland was raised to 0.35 Fmk per kg from 15 June 1991 and to 0.60 Fmk per kg from 15 August 1991. This tax is used to help offset the cost of subsidising exports. A new tax on fertilisers has been proposed for 1992. It would replace the present taxes and consist of a tax of 1.70 Fmk per kg of phosphorus and 2.90 Fmk per kg of nitrogen, which corresponds to an average rate of 0.60 Fmk per kg of fertiliser. Bearing in mind the seasonal pricing of fertiliser it would add between 32.8 to 37.3 per cent to the basic price of fertiliser, depending on the time of year.

The European Community

An intensive debate on the future of the European Community's Common Agricultural Policy (CAP) was initiated in 1991. At the beginning of the year the Commission set out its reflections on the current state of the CAP and the need for change. Central to the Commission's paper was the argument that the system of price guarantees had led to growing output, surpluses and rapidly rising budgetary expenditure, mostly devoted to a small proportion of the Community's farms. Furthermore, the Commission suggested that the incentives to increase output and intensify production were putting the environment at increasing risk. It was recognised that changes to the CAP should address the environmental role of agriculture as well as questions of controlling output, stabilising the budget, etc. On the basis of this analysis, the Commission proposed a significant number of measures to reform the CAP, first in February 1991 and later in July 1991 in a Communication entitled *"The Development and Future of the Common Agricultural Policy"* (COM(91)258 Final). The proposals cover most of the main sectors of production in the Community, together accounting for about three-quarters of the total value of EC agricultural output subject to the CAP. Reductions in prices are proposed for several commodities, most notably for cereals where a cut of about 35 per cent is suggested. Cereal producers would be compensated by a new system of direct payments which would include a link with set-aside, which would be obligatory for larger farmers if they are to qualify for compensation. In the livestock sector some reductions in prices are proposed as well and a new system of compensatory payments per head of livestock would be introduced which would include limitations on the numbers eligible and upper limits on the livestock density on farms qualifying for compensation. In most sectors, the new compensatory measures would be "modulated" in favour of smaller producers.

Alongside changes in the main commodity regimes, the Commission proposed three significant accompanying measures. One is a new system of incentives for older farmers who retire early, another is an enhanced aid regime for afforestation and a third is an agri-environmental action programme. Together these three measures are estimated to be likely to require some four billion ECU in expenditure from the Community agriculture budget over a five year period. The agri-environment measures would extend the Community's existing schemes for aiding extensification and environmentally sensitive farming systems and add new elements such as assistance for long-term set-aside for environmental reasons, incentives for the upkeep of abandoned farmland and woodlands and new education and training schemes for farmers. Farmers would receive incentives either to reduce substantially their use of fertilisers and/or pesticides or to maintain reductions which they had made already. There would be parallel incentives to reduce sheep and cattle numbers on farms. Member States would be obliged to introduce schemes of this kind, at least within certain zones, but participation by farmers would be voluntary. Detailed schemes would be drawn up at regional or national level and not centrally by the Community.

Switzerland

At the end of 1991, the Federal Council implemented an ordinance on the orientation of plant production and extensive farming. Its aim is to decrease cereal acreage and encourage farmers to farm the land less intensively in a more site-oriented and environment-friendly way. Contemplated measures include, among others, payments for the reallocation of rotated acreages to ecological "compensation" or green fallow for extensive cereal crops and pasturing.

In the 7th Report on Agriculture, which was published in January 1992, the Federal Council describes the new orientation of the Swiss agricultural policy. One of its central objectives is "production that safeguards the environment". It is proposed to strengthen the ecological orientation of agricultural policy through targeted measures stimulating, for example, farm extensification and environment-friendly farming methods. The reallocation of farm acreage to other uses such as ecological "compensation" is encouraged if it is deemed appropriate and economically justified.

The first practical step taken under this policy is a modification of the Agricultural Act, enabling payments for the adoption of farming methods which would safeguard the environment and animals (integrated production, biological agriculture, special ecological services). This modification has been submitted to Parliament.

All these measures were designed so as not to promote increased production.

Denmark

An Action Plan for a Sustainable Development in Agriculture was published in April 1991. In December 1991 the competent Parliamentary Committee presented its report on the Action Plan. The plan is now in the process of implementation.

In order to improve the utilization of livestock manure the Action Plan for a Sustainable Development in Agriculture contains, *inter alia*, the following measures:

- Slurry/liquid manure may not be spread in the autumn except in September for winter rape and grass. The situation will be reviewed in the spring of 1997 at the latest;
- Slurry/liquid manure shall be spread on growing crops or be injected directly into the soil;
- Solid manure must be ploughed in immediately after spreading; and
- Solid manure may not be spread on fields in the autumn before 20th October except for fields which will subsequently have a green cover.

In order to comply with the rules concerning the application of livestock manure, farms are required to have the necessary storage capacity. As a minimum they are required to have capacity for 6 months.

In Denmark the possibility of a fertilizer tax has also been considered. However, the idea has been rejected because of the lack of effectiveness in a number of cases of a tax which would be imposed on an input factor and not on the loss of nitrogen. Furthermore, the level of the tax would have to be quite considerable. This would have serious, undesirable consequences with regard to production patterns and income levels. Instead a regulatory system controlling, *inter alia*, the utilization of manure will be implemented by August 1993.

Each year farmers shall send in key figures concerning their use of manure and fertilizers to the authorities in order to show that rates requiring a certain utilization of nitrogen in manure have been met. These figures are subsequently controlled by the authorities.

The existing grant scheme for the construction of storage capacity will be continued.

With a view to protecting vulnerable groundwater resources, approximately 50 000 ha of land in three counties in Jutland shall be designated as environmentally sensitive areas and farmers in these areas compensated if they agree to reduce fertilization and the use of pesticides.

Possibilities to increase denitrification in meadows will be explored.

To reduce the use of pesticides the following measures will be introduced:

– Research will be carried out in order to extend and develop integrated plant production systems;
– To help farmers cut their use of pesticides, advisory activities will be reinforced;
– All users of pesticides shall undergo special training courses;
– Public random control of pesticide spraying equipment will be established;
– Farmers shall keep a record of their use of pesticides;
– Before July 1992 the Government shall present an account of the possibilities of establishing more precise evaluation criteria to ensure quicker implementation of the more rigorous requirements applying to pesticides (*e.g.* by speeding up the ongoing re-evaluation process). The repeal of the objectives of the 1986 Pesticide Action Plan to halve the frequency of treatment depends on the establishment of more environmentally relevant and exact evaluation criteria.

Proposals concerning protection of nature and landscape through, *inter alia*, mandatory 2 meter non-cultivated filter strips along water courses and lakes were adopted by Parliament in December 1991.

MAIN SALES OUTLETS OF OECD PUBLICATIONS
PRINCIPAUX POINTS DE VENTE DES PUBLICATIONS DE L'OCDE

ARGENTINA – ARGENTINE
Carlos Hirsch S.R.L.
Galería Güemes, Florida 165, 4° Piso
1333 Buenos Aires   Tel. (1) 331.1787 y 331.2391
Telefax: (1) 331.1787

AUSTRALIA – AUSTRALIE
D.A. Information Services
648 Whitehorse Road, P.O.B 163
Mitcham, Victoria 3132   Tel. (03) 873.4411
Telefax: (03) 873.5679

AUSTRIA – AUTRICHE
Gerold & Co.
Graben 31
Wien I   Tel. (0222) 533.50.14

BELGIUM – BELGIQUE
Jean De Lannoy
Avenue du Roi 202
B-1060 Bruxelles   Tel. (02) 538.51.69/538.08.41
Telefax: (02) 538.08.41

CANADA
Renouf Publishing Company Ltd.
1294 Algoma Road
Ottawa, ON K1B 3W8   Tel. (613) 741.4333
Telefax: (613) 741.5439
Stores:
61 Sparks Street
Ottawa, ON K1P 5R1   Tel. (613) 238.8985
211 Yonge Street
Toronto, ON M5B 1M4   Tel. (416) 363.3171
Les Éditions La Liberté Inc.
3020 Chemin Sainte-Foy
Sainte-Foy, PQ G1X 3V6   Tel. (418) 658.3763
Telefax: (418) 658.3763

Federal Publications
165 University Avenue
Toronto, ON M5H 3B8   Tel. (416) 581.1552
Telefax: (416) 581.1743

CHINA – CHINE
China National Publications Import
Export Corporation (CNPIEC)
16 Gongti E. Road, Chaoyang District
P.O. Box 88 or 50
Beijing 100704 PR   Tel. (01) 506.6688
Telefax: (01) 506.3101

DENMARK – DANEMARK
Munksgaard Export and Subscription Service
35, Nørre Søgade, P.O. Box 2148
DK-1016 København K   Tel. (33) 12.85.70
Telefax: (33) 12.93.87

FINLAND – FINLANDE
Akateeminen Kirjakauppa
Keskuskatu 1, P.O. Box 128
00100 Helsinki   Tel. (358 0) 12141
Telefax: (358 0) 121.4441

FRANCE
OECD/OCDE
Mail Orders/Commandes par correspondance:
2, rue André-Pascal
75775 Paris Cedex 16   Tel. (33-1) 45.24.82.00
Telefax: (33-1) 45.24.85.00   or (33-1) 45.24.81.76
Telex: 640048 OCDE
OECD Bookshop/Librairie de l'OCDE :
33, rue Octave-Feuillet
75016 Paris   Tel. (33-1) 45.24.81.67
(33-1) 45.24.81.81
Documentation Française
29, quai Voltaire
75007 Paris   Tel. 40.15.70.00
Gibert Jeune (Droit-Économie)
6, place Saint-Michel
75006 Paris   Tel. 43.25.91.19

Librairie du Commerce International
10, avenue d'Iéna
75016 Paris   Tel. 40.73.34.60
Librairie Dunod
Université Paris-Dauphine
Place du Maréchal de Lattre de Tassigny
75016 Paris   Tel. 47.27.18.56
Librairie Lavoisier
11, rue Lavoisier
75008 Paris   Tel. 42.65.39.95
Librairie L.G.D.J. - Montchrestien
20, rue Soufflot
75005 Paris   Tel. 46.33.89.85
Librairie des Sciences Politiques
30, rue Saint-Guillaume
75007 Paris   Tel. 45.48.36.02
P.U.F.
49, boulevard Saint-Michel
75005 Paris   Tel. 43.25.83.40
Librairie de l'Université
12a, rue Nazareth
13100 Aix-en-Provence   Tel. (16) 42.26.18.08
Documentation Française
165, rue Garibaldi
69003 Lyon   Tel. (16) 78.63.32.23
Librairie Decitre
29, place Bellecour
69002 Lyon   Tel. (16) 72.40.54.54

GERMANY – ALLEMAGNE
OECD Publications and Information Centre
Schedestrasse 7
D-W 5300 Bonn 1   Tel. (0228) 21.60.45
Telefax: (0228) 26.11.04

GREECE – GRÈCE
Librairie Kauffmann
Mavrokordatou 9
106 78 Athens   Tel. 322.21.60
Telefax: 363.39.67

HONG-KONG
Swindon Book Co. Ltd.
13–15 Lock Road
Kowloon, Hong Kong   Tel. 366.80.31
Telefax: 739.49.75

ICELAND – ISLANDE
Mál Mog Menning
Laugavegi 18, Pósthólf 392
121 Reykjavik   Tel. 162.35.23

INDIA – INDE
Oxford Book and Stationery Co.
Scindia House
New Delhi 110001   Tel.(11) 331.5896/5308
Telefax: (11) 332.5993
17 Park Street
Calcutta 700016   Tel. 240832

INDONESIA – INDONÉSIE
Pdii-Lipi
P.O. Box 269/JKSMG/88
Jakarta 12790   Tel. 583467
Telex: 62 875

IRELAND – IRLANDE
TDC Publishers – Library Suppliers
12 North Frederick Street
Dublin 1   Tel. 74.48.35/74.96.77
Telefax: 74.84.16

ISRAEL
Electronic Publications only
Publications électroniques seulement
Sophist Systems Ltd.
71 Allenby Street
Tel-Aviv 65134   Tel. 3-29.00.21
Telefax: 3-29.92.39

ITALY – ITALIE
Libreria Commissionaria Sansoni
Via Duca di Calabria 1/1
50125 Firenze   Tel. (055) 64.54.15
Telefax: (055) 64.12.57
Via Bartolini 29
20155 Milano   Tel. (02) 36.50.83
Editrice e Libreria Herder
Piazza Montecitorio 120
00186 Roma   Tel. 679.46.28
Telefax: 678.47.51
Libreria Hoepli
Via Hoepli 5
20121 Milano   Tel. (02) 86.54.46
Telefax: (02) 805.28.86
Libreria Scientifica
Dott. Lucio de Biasio 'Aeiou'
Via Coronelli, 6
20146 Milano   Tel. (02) 48.95.45.52
Telefax: (02) 48.95.45.48

JAPAN – JAPON
OECD Publications and Information Centre
Landic Akasaka Building
2-3-4 Akasaka, Minato-ku
Tokyo 107   Tel. (81.3) 3586.2016
Telefax: (81.3) 3584.7929

KOREA – CORÉE
Kyobo Book Centre Co. Ltd.
P.O. Box 1658, Kwang Hwa Moon
Seoul   Tel. 730.78.91
Telefax: 735.00.30

MALAYSIA – MALAISIE
Co-operative Bookshop Ltd.
University of Malaya
P.O. Box 1127, Jalan Pantai Baru
59700 Kuala Lumpur
Malaysia   Tel. 756.5000/756.5425
Telefax: 757.3661

NETHERLANDS – PAYS-BAS
SDU Uitgeverij
Christoffel Plantijnstraat 2
Postbus 20014
2500 EA's-Gravenhage   Tel. (070 3) 78.99.11
Voor bestellingen: Tel. (070 3) 78.98.80
Telefax: (070 3) 47.63.51

**NEW ZEALAND
NOUVELLE-ZÉLANDE**
Legislation Services
P.O. Box 12418
Thorndon, Wellington   Tel. (04) 496.5652
Telefax: (04) 496.5698

NORWAY – NORVÈGE
Narvesen Info Center – NIC
Bertrand Narvesens vei 2
P.O. Box 6125 Etterstad
0602 Oslo 6   Tel. (02) 57.33.00
Telefax: (02) 68.19.01

PAKISTAN
Mirza Book Agency
65 Shahrah Quaid-E-Azam
Lahore 3   Tel. 66.839
Telex: 44886 UBL PK. Attn: MIRZA BK

PORTUGAL
Livraria Portugal
Rua do Carmo 70-74
Apart. 2681
1117 Lisboa Codex   Tel.: (01) 347.49.82/3/4/5
Telefax: (01) 347.02.64

OECD PUBLICATIONS, 2 rue André-Pascal, 75775 PARIS CEDEX 16
PRINTED IN FRANCE
(97 92 11 1) ISBN 92-64-13820-X - No. 46281 1993